HIPPIE LANE

THE COOKBOOK

HIPPIE LANE

THE COOKBOOK

Taline Gabrielian

Photography by Petrina Tinslay,
Sneh Roy and Omid Daghighi

MURDOCH BOOKS

SYDNEY · LONDON

CONTENTS

The Hippie Lane Philosophy 7

The Essentials 8

THE HIPPIE LANE PHILOSOPHY

Food has always played a leading role in my life. My family is of Armenian heritage and coming together around the dining table for a home-cooked meal was the norm. I was exposed to good food from an early age and I learnt to appreciate the value of cooking and how it brings people together. My fondest memories are of my mother gathering close friends and family to experience her fab feasts. The smell, the laughter, the shared stories... The best experiences, all kept in my heart.

I began to cook in my teens. I loved flicking through cookbooks and found endless inspiration. It fired my imagination and gave me an appetite for beautifully presented meals.

When I reached adulthood, I became interested in health and learning more about natural vs processed foods, and about how our food choices impact our wellbeing and overall health. When I learnt that I had some common food intolerances (to dairy, wheat and eggs), it took my interest in all things food and health to a new level. I began researching everyday ingredients and the effects they can have on our health — it totally changed how I view food. I adopted an organic wholefood diet and became far more mindful about what I was putting in my body.

I started experimenting with a variety of less commonly known ingredients, including gluten-free grains, raw foods, superfoods and natural plant-based ingredients. I fell in love with the tastes and textures that resulted from this delicious period of experimentation, and became obsessed with creating recipes that nourished my family. This is how Hippie Lane came to life.

What diet am I on? I'm not. I don't do diets. My belief is that we have an evolving relationship with food and, during different stages of life, we adopt different habits. I let my body direct me. Right now, I'm eating a majority of plant-based meals, but I don't classify myself as fully plant based, vegan, vegetarian or raw. Food must be enjoyed and appreciated, and when we label ourselves and become inflexible about our choices, I feel it takes away a great source of joy from life.

My passion for healthy, wholesome food is all encompassing. It gets me out of bed in the morning, gives me limitless energy in the kitchen and pushes me to continue to create. I'm in my element creating recipes. It's where I let go. Aside from the delicious results, I find it therapeutic... there are no rules and I just let it flow.

My goal is to inspire a healthy approach to eating – one that is less reliant on animal products and more centred around food that is fresh and whole, from the earth.

This book is about embracing our love affair with food and the traditions that give us so much pleasure: the daily breakfast, the morning smoothie, the birthday gathering, Friday-night dinner date or Sunday brunch. It is about honouring and revitalising those food rituals.

Sharing a nourishing meal with family and friends is my ultimate happy place. I invite you to join me in that magical space, and share it in your own home with your own family and friends.

The essentials
INGREDIENTS

Acai powder

Pronounced *ah-sah-ee*, acai powder is the star ingredient in my fave breakfast, the acai bowl. Native to the Amazon, the dark purple acai berry is one of the richest known natural sources of antioxidants, and is also packed full of essential vitamins, minerals and dietary fibre. Combined with frozen fruit, it makes a deliciously simple and supercharged breakfast bowl. I'm obsessed!

Activated buckwheat groats

An absolute godsend to gluten-free people around the world! Deliciously crunchy and versatile, activated buckwheat can be used in so many ways. You can use it as a granola or cereal replacement for breakfast, or add some to smoothie bowls for crunch. I include it in the base of cheesecakes or slices, and my raw breakfast sprinkles (page 48), and it works beautifully.

You'll find activated buckwheat in health food stores and online, or you can make your own by following these simple steps: soak 180 g (6½ oz/1 cup) raw buckwheat groats overnight in 500 ml (17 fl oz/2 cups) filtered water mixed with 1 teaspoon salt. Rinse and drain. Set a food dehydrator to 40°C (105°F), spread the groats on your dehydrating trays and leave for 24–48 hours, or until dry and crisp. Alternatively, spread the groats on a baking tray lined with baking paper and dry in the oven at its lowest setting for 24–48 hours, or until dry and crisp. Easy peasy!

Almond meal

Almond meal is simply made by grinding almonds. Super delicious in baked goods, it adds a nutty, moist texture and beautiful flavour to recipes. Almonds are well known for their healthy fats, fibre, protein, magnesium and vitamin E; health benefits may include lowering blood sugar levels, blood pressure and cholesterol. To maintain freshness, keep your almond meal in the fridge in an airtight container.

Berry powders

I've recently discovered blueberry and strawberry fruit powders and am completely in love! Full of antioxidants, berry powders are not only delicious, but nutritious. I use them in smoothies, stir them through breakfast dishes, and sprinkle them on almost everything. You'll find them in good health food stores and online.

Buckwheat flour

I'm a big fan of buckwheat. I love it in its natural form, as activated groats, and when ground into a flour. Although its name suggests it is a form of wheat, buckwheat is classified as a seed, and is naturally gluten free. Low in fat, it contains disease-fighting antioxidants and highly digestible protein, as well as many vitamins and minerals. With its deliciously nutty flavour, buckwheat flour is the star ingredient in my favourite pancakes and baked cinnamon donuts. A definite pantry staple.

Cacao butter

One of the most stable fats around, cacao butter is the pure, cold-pressed oil of the cacao bean and provides a healthy dose of omega-6 and omega-9 fatty acids. I use it in place of coconut oil in some of my cakes, and for making chocolate. Cacao butter is solid, but I always use it in liquid form. To liquefy cacao butter, simply place it in a heatproof bowl over a saucepan of simmering water and stir it with a whisk or a spatula, checking with a thermometer to ensure the temperature does not rise above 48°C (118°F), to keep all the valuable nutrients intact. If it starts rising above this temperature, remove the bowl from the heat; the cacao butter will be warm enough to finish melting on its own.

Cacao powder, raw

If you want serious nutrition, raw cacao powder is where it's at! Unlike regular cocoa powder, which is heat-treated, raw cacao powder is made by cold-pressing unroasted cacao beans. This process removes the fat, while keeping all its nutrients and enzymes intact. I use dark organic cacao powder in most of my recipes.

Cashews

Raw organic cashews contain a host of vitamins and minerals, including copper, magnesium, manganese, phosphorus, vitamin K and oleic acid. Together these nutrients promote bone strength and joint flexibility, may help discourage migraines, improve memory, lower blood pressure, and help protect against UV damage, heart disease and cancer.

I use cashews in many of my raw cakes and savoury sauces. I soak them in water overnight for maximum nutrient absorption. If you are running short of time, you can speed up the process by soaking them in boiling water for 30–60 minutes.

Chia seeds

Gluten free, and super high in omega-3 fatty acids, chia seeds are full of nutrition, unbelievably versatile and an essential pantry staple. I soak them to make breakfast puddings, and have them in muesli mixes, bliss balls, and in raw and baked treats. High in fibre, protein and calcium, they keep you regular and fully satisfied. You'll find them in major supermarkets.

Coconut, dried

Dried coconut plays a starring role in many of my breakfast and treat recipes. I can't look past it, as it is so versatile, as well as totally delicious. Coconut also boasts many health benefits, mainly due to its high levels of lauric acid, an anti-fungal, anti-viral compound thought to be helpful for gut health and immunity.

Shredded coconut is made from coconut flesh that has simply been dried and shredded. I love its texture in raw treats and as a breakfast topper.

Flaked coconut is basically the same as shredded, but processed into flatter pieces, making it less stringy. Desiccated coconut is also dried, but contains less moisture than shredded or flaked coconut. Finer in texture, it works beautifully in raw and baked treats.

Coconut butter

A creamy, velvety spread made by blending coconut flesh, coconut butter is rich in immunity-boosting lauric acid. It may also help increase your metabolism, enhancing energy levels and aiding in weight loss. I love using it in frostings. You can find it in health stores and online.

Coconut cream & coconut milk

I use coconut milk in many recipes for its creamy texture and distinctive flavour. Coconut milk is the liquid that comes from the grated flesh of a coconut, which is processed with water to create a milk. I often use it in combination with other plant milks, such as rice or almond milk, as they blend beautifully together. Coconut cream contains less water than coconut milk, resulting in a much thicker texture.

Most tinned coconut milks include an emulsifier; I use brands that are 100% organic and BPA free. You could also use long-life coconut milk if you wish.

Coconut flour

Coconut flour is made from grinding coconut pulp after it has been squeezed for coconut milk. It contains much of the fibre from the coconut, and absorbs lots of liquid. High in protein, it is particularly handy as a thickener, and simply for its delicious nutty flavour. I add some to my pancake mix to give it a little extra rise. It is naturally sweet and filling, which is an extra bonus.

Coconut oil

Possibly the most versatile oil on earth, coconut oil is a definite keeper. With its high smoke point, coconut oil can be used at high temperatures without becoming unstable and losing its anti-inflammatory and antioxidant nutrients. I use it in much of my savoury cooking, as well as raw and baked treats. For maximum health and taste benefits, use cold-pressed (and preferably organic) coconut oil.

Coconut oil solidifies in colder temperatures. To liquefy it to use in recipes, immerse your jar in a bowl of boiling water. Within a few minutes, the oil will begin to melt. Keep it immersed a little longer for the oil to melt completely.

Coconut sugar

Coconut sugar (also known as coco sugar or coconut palm sugar) is a natural sugar produced from the sap of cut flower buds of the coconut palm. This tasty sugar is considered the most sustainably produced. Being high in sucrose, I wouldn't call coconut sugar a health food, but it does offer some trace nutrients, and has a less dramatic impact on blood sugar than many other natural sweeteners.

Coconut yoghurt

Irresistibly creamy, full of flavour and totally satisfying, coconut yoghurt is my favourite dairy-free yoghurt. I can't get enough of it. Consumed in moderation, it can benefit your health and help fight infection. It is made from coconut cream and is sold in major supermarkets and health food stores — or make your own following my simple tip on page 62.

Dates, medjool and pitted

Dates are a must in your pantry. I often use medjool and sometimes pitted dates in my recipes. Medjool are the larger fresh dates you'll find in the fruit and veg section of your grocery store. They're soft and super sweet, and perfect in shakes, smoothies and raw treats. They contain pits, which need to be removed before consuming.

Pitted dates are the dried variety most commonly found in the baking or dried fruit section of grocery stores. They are chewier and less moist than fresh dates, and ideal for baking.

Grapeseed oil

When pan-frying, I often use grapeseed oil for its mild flavour and high smoke point. The 'smoke point' is the temperature at which an oil will begin to smoke. When heated past its smoke point, the fat in the oil starts to break down, releasing toxic fumes and free radicals (nasty). Although we most often cook at moderate temperatures and the risk of heating the oil past its smoke point is unlikely, I like to play it safe.

Linseed meal

Also called flaxseeds, linseeds are one of the leading sources of plant-derived omega-3 fatty acids and dietary fibre. Ground linseeds are incredibly useful in plant-based baking as an egg substitute. When linseeds are ground and mixed with water, they thicken and act as a binding agent, and are commonly called a 'flax egg'. Fortunately, linseed meal is easily processed by the body and provides many health benefits. Grinding your own linseed meal as you need it yields the best binding results; I store mine in the fridge to keep it as fresh as possible.

Lucuma powder

A natural sweetener prepared from the Peruvian lucuma fruit. Known as 'Incan gold', the pulp of the fruit is dehydrated to produce the powder, which is commonly added to smoothies, treats and breakfast foods. In recipes it is generally interchangeable with mesquite powder — they both offer a caramel-like flavour and contain a heap of nutrients.

Maca powder

Maca is a root plant known for its energising and revitalising properties. Often referred to as 'Peruvian ginseng', maca powder is nutritionally dense, containing vitamins, minerals, enzymes and amino acids. Loaded with vitamin C and iron, maca can help boost the immune system for daily wellness, and also help with stress, mood, PMS and menopausal symptoms. I add a teaspoon to smoothies or treats when I need an energy boost. However, too much maca can cause hormonal disruption and other side effects, and should be avoided altogether by people with thyroid illnesses. Check with your doctor or naturopath if you have concerns.

Mesquite powder

Mesquite is a nutritious superfood powder with a sweet, rich, nutty, caramel flavour that works beautifully in smoothies and treats. The powder is extracted by grinding the seed pods of the mesquite plant, commonly found in South America. It is high in protein, and rich in calcium, magnesium, iron, zinc and dietary fibre. I buy mine from good health food stores and online.

Millet

One of the world's oldest crops, millet is a nutty, mildly sweet grain, once mainly used as bird and livestock feed. Increased interest in its nutritional and gluten-free properties has revitalised its image, and it is now enjoyed as a wheat-free alternative. I use millet flakes in my Banana and maple bread (page 36). It has a mild flavour that pairs well with most foods. Millet contains B group vitamins, magnesium, potassium and dietary fibre, and may assist with toxin excretion. Adding millet to your diet while detoxing can help speed up the process.

Nut butter

Nut butter is an addictive spread achieved by grinding nuts into a paste. I use nut butter a lot in my recipes — and I often eat it straight out of the jar with a spoon! Nut butters can be found in most supermarkets and health food stores; to make your own, see my recipes on pages 66–67.

Nutritional yeast

Besides its delicious cheesy taste, nutritional yeast (also called savoury yeast flakes) is very nutritious, as its name would suggest. It is high in some B-complex vitamins, and is often fortified with B12. It is also a complete protein, low in fat and sodium, is free of sugar and gluten, and contains iron. Yes to all! I'm addicted to the stuff, and add it to cashew-based sauces and cheeses. You'll find it in most health food stores, some supermarkets and online.

Oats

Oats have got to be the ideal breakfast comfort food, and add a subtle, delicious flavour to cookies, baked goods and raw treats. Much controversy surrounds the presence of gluten in oats, and whether gluten-free oats exist. I've done the research and found that oats are naturally gluten free, but are almost always contaminated during the milling process. Oats contain a protein called avenin, which can produce a gluten-like reaction in some people with coeliac disease.

Food Standards Australia New Zealand prohibits any form of oat being labelled as gluten-free in Australia or New Zealand, but a few international brands sell gluten-free oats that have been tested to not contain gluten.

While oats most often do not cause a reaction for people with an intolerance or sensitivity to gluten, the Coeliac Australia society does not recommend that people with coeliac disease consume oats of any kind.

If oats are a concern, you can almost always substitute them in my recipes with quinoa flakes.

Olive oil

Used heavily in Mediterranean cooking, and in my own cooking! Please pay attention to the quality of the oil you use. Extra virgin olive oil is the purest grade you can get. It is made by crushing olives and cold-extracting the juice, without altering the oil in any way, and using no additives during the process. Naturally, it has the finest flavour and more health benefits. The phenolic compounds in olive oil have been found to promote cardiovascular and digestive health, and have anti-inflammatory and cancer-fighting qualities.

The more processed and refined your olive oil is, the less beneficial it will be.

Potato flour

Potato flour is made from cooked, dried and ground potatoes. It works well with other gluten-free flours and adds a desirable moist, soft texture to pancakes and cupcakes. Don't confuse it with potato starch. Ground from the whole potatoes, including the skin, potato flour is heavier and denser than potato starch and tastes more like potato. Potato starch is flavourless and is better used as a thickener.

Psyllium husks

Mainly used as a form of natural dietary fibre, psyllium husks are often sprinkled on breakfast bowls or added to smoothies. I find psyllium adds a beneficial texture to gluten-free baking in general, making the result more moist and tender. Psyllium is readily available in supermarkets and health food stores.

Quinoa

I'm obsessed with quinoa. I love its taste and texture, and that it's high in protein, less starchy than rice, and so versatile. I often use quinoa flakes in baked goods and savoury patties, the cooked grain in salads and meals, and quinoa puffs in sweet treats. Quinoa is gluten-free, but if you are highly sensitive to gluten, ensure the quinoa you buy hasn't been processed in a facility that also processes grains, to avoid any potential gluten cross-contamination.

Rice malt syrup

Organic brown rice malt syrup is a naturally malted whole-grain sweetener derived from brown rice. Characteristically rich but mildly flavoured, it complements other flavours in a recipe, whereas sweeteners such as honey, maple syrup and molasses have a stronger, more distinctive flavour.

If you can't find brown rice malt syrup, use pure Canadian maple syrup. It contains a decent amount of some minerals, especially manganese and zinc. Make sure you buy 100% Canadian maple syrup and not the cheaper maple-flavoured syrups, which are often made from a nasty mix of sugar, corn syrup, molasses, caramel colour, alcohol, vanilla extract, flavours and a sulphite-based preservative.

Sorghum flour

A popular option for gluten-free baking, sorghum flour is ground from wholegrain sorghum, and has a light texture and mild sweet flavour. Being high in fibre, it promotes digestive health, helps fight cardiovascular disease and aids in blood sugar control.

Used alone, sorghum flour produces dry, gritty, baked goods. I combine it with tapioca starch and rice flour to give my baked gluten-free recipes better volume and texture.

Tapioca flour

Tapioca flour, also called tapioca starch, adds structure to gluten-free baking. It comes from the root of the cassava plant, and in combination with other gluten-free flours, provides a chewy texture to baked goods.

Tapioca flour is similar to arrowroot powder, but also gives a little elasticity to baked items.

Teff flour

Like quinoa, teff is a really handy and nutritious gluten-free grain. Long a nourishing staple of highland Ethiopians, the grain may be the tiniest in the world, but packs in many health benefits. Teff is high in protein, iron and calcium, and contains all nine essential amino acids. It is excellent for maintaining blood sugar balance and feeding the friendly bacteria in the gut, for improved digestive health. I use ivory teff flour in my baked cinnamon donuts and it works a treat. Available online and in health food stores.

Vanilla powder

Organic vanilla powder is such a beautiful product, I can't recommend it highly enough. It is simply made from grinding organically grown vanilla beans to a powder — and nothing else! Its aroma and taste is far superior to extracts and essences, particularly in smoothies and raw cakes and slices.

You can make your own vanilla powder by simply grinding some organic vanilla bean pods in a coffee or nut grinder.

The next best thing is organic vanilla bean paste or extract. Most pastes and extracts contain some kind of added sugar, but there are a few superior products that don't, so check the label.

Xanthan gum

Made from the outer layer of a tiny, inactive bacterium called *Xanthomonas campestris*, xanthan gum is commonly used in gluten-free baking as a binding agent. I use it as an emulsifier, and to add volume to gluten-free batters.

Za'atar

A tangy Middle Eastern spice mixture that includes dried thyme and oregano, ground sumac, sesame seeds and salt. I blend za'atar with olive oil and add it to a cauliflower 'dough' to create my gluten-free *mana'eesh* 'flatbread' — a staple of mine growing up.

In Middle Eastern culture, za'atar is believed to give strength and clear the mind. It is also said to boost the immune system and circulation, build strong bones, soothe inflammation, boost energy and improve mood.

The essentials
EQUIPMENT

Food processor

If there's one thing I can't live without, it's my food processor. You'll notice it appears countless times in my recipes. It is everything to me! A reliable food processor makes my raw cakes possible. It's also a lifeline for making pesto, hummus and other dips, cauliflower 'rice', and for simply grating or finely slicing vegies. I use one with multiple bowls for larger or smaller batches, and a full selection of cutting and grating blades. It's simple and straight to the point with just three functions — just how I like it.

Spiraliser or julienne vegetable peeler

A spiraliser produces large batches of vegie noodles effortlessly. A simple and inexpensive julienne vegetable peeler or slicer also does the job, but takes a bit longer.

High-speed blender

I use a high-speed blender for sauces, dips, soups, most of my salad dressings, as well as all the lush smoothies, creamy ice creams, fruity ice pops and nut milks. It's also useful for achieving a super-smooth texture for creamy 'cheesecake' fillings. You'll notice that in some of my recipes I transfer some cheeses from a food processor to a blender for an extra-smooth finish.

Baking tins

The Sweet Fix chapter (where all the fun is at!) requires you to have a small collection of baking tins. Within each recipe I've given some approximate tin sizes, but a few centimetres over or under won't cause any dramas, so don't get too hung up on my suggestions. A few standard-sized loaf (bar) tins, along with some rectangular, circular and square tins, is really about all you'll need to get going.

Nutrition codes

R raw + The ingredients are not heated above 48°C (117°F), keeping valuable nutrients and enzymes intact

VGN vegan + Contains no animal products or byproducts, including honey, dairy or eggs

DF dairy-free + Contains no ingredients derived from animal milks, including butter and dairy-based milk, cream, yoghurt and cheese

GF gluten-free + Does not contain gluten, a protein found in wheat, barley, rye, triticale, malt and brewer's yeast

RSF refined sugar-free + Does not contain highly refined white sugar, but may contain other less-refined sweeteners with a lower GI, such as rice malt syrup, dates or coconut sugar

NF nut-free + Does not contain nuts or nut products

RISE
+
SHINE

Acai, you sexy thing! Hawaii is where I first discovered acai, and where my love affair with it began. After eating too many super-sweet acai bowls, I kept trialling different combinations until I landed this one. Peanut butter and cacao add a creamy body to the fruity base, boosting its nutritional value to powerhouse level.

I can't put into words how much I love this acai recipe. It's not your traditional acai bowl, but try it, enjoy it and thank me later.

Peanut butter acai bowl with RAWnola

SERVES 1 ✕ R + VGN + DF + GF + RSF

1 chopped banana, frozen
125 g (4½ oz/1 cup) frozen mixed berries
1 tablespoon acai powder
1 tablespoon raw cacao powder
1 tablespoon peanut butter (see tip), plus extra to serve
125 ml (4 fl oz/½ cup) coconut water
125 ml (4 fl oz/½ cup) rice milk or almond milk
50 g (1¾ oz/½ cup) RAWnola (page 32)
seasonal fresh fruit, to serve

Place all the ingredients, except the RAWnola and fresh fruit, in a high-speed blender. Pulse until you've reached a soft-serve consistency. You want a semi-frozen finish, so resist adding more liquid; instead, use the blender stick to force the frozen fruit onto the blades to help it break down.

Spoon into a bowl and top with the RAWnola, fruit and other toppings of your choice. Add an extra dollop of peanut butter and dig in.

TIP *For a nut-free option, use tahini instead of peanut butter.*

*Bursting with flavour and health benefits, these
deliciously simple overnight oats are on high rotation
in our household. Oats are a filling breakfast option and
provide plenty of fibre and B vitamins, boosted with all
the nourishing goodness of chia and sesame seeds.*

*Throw it all together before you go to bed, then wake
up to a cafe-style breakfast the whole family will enjoy.*

Apple & coconut overnight oats

SERVES 4 ✪ R + VGN + DF + GF + RSF + NF

Place the oats, chia seeds and
sesame seeds in a bowl. Add the
yoghurt and apple juice and mix well.
Stir in the cinnamon, then cover and
place in the fridge overnight.

Serve topped with the apple,
coconut and passionfruit pulp, and a
sprinkling of microgreens if desired.

TIP *If you find your oats are slightly
dry in the morning, stir in an extra
dollop of coconut yoghurt for
added creaminess.*

90 g (3¼ oz/1 cup) gluten-free rolled
   (porridge) oats
1 tablespoon chia seeds
1 tablespoon sesame seeds
420 g (15 oz/1½ cups) coconut yoghurt
125 ml (4 fl oz/½ cup) apple juice
1 teaspoon ground cinnamon
1 apple, shredded or grated
2 tablespoons shredded coconut
pulp of 2 passionfruit
microgreens, to garnish (optional)

Chia is a versatile, powerful little seed with outstanding health benefits. It is very high in calcium, and being high in fibre it keeps you feeling full for longer and is especially handy for regularity. It is also gluten, wheat and nut free. I love it in these puddings, which are perfect any time of the day.

These three puddings can be enjoyed individually, or layered into a glass serving jar for a neapolitan effect.

Neapolitan chia puddings

EACH PUDDING SERVES 2

R + VGN + DF + GF + RSF

To make the chocolate chia, place the chia seeds in a bowl with the coconut milk and whisk together with a fork. Add the cacao, lucuma and rice malt syrup and whisk well. Set in the fridge for up to 8 hours, or overnight, before serving with your favourite topping.

To make the caramel chia, place the chia seeds in a bowl with the coconut or almond milk and whisk together with a fork. Add the mesquite powder and rice malt syrup and whisk well. Set in the fridge for at least 8 hours, or overnight, before serving with your favourite topping.

To make the strawberry chia, place the chia seeds in a bowl with the almond milk and whisk together with a fork. Set in the fridge for at least 8 hours, or overnight. When you're ready to serve, place the strawberries, vanilla and rice malt syrup in a blender and whiz into a purée on high speed. Add the purée to the chia seeds and whisk well. Spoon into serving glasses, add your favourite topping and serve immediately.

***TIP** To make these puddings nut free, use coconut milk instead of almond milk.*

Chocolate chia

40 g (1½ oz/¼ cup) chia seeds
375 ml (13 fl oz/1½ cups) coconut milk
1 tablespoon raw cacao powder
1 teaspoon lucuma powder
1–2 teaspoons rice malt syrup

Caramel chia

40 g (1½ oz/¼ cup) chia seeds
375 ml (13 fl oz/1½ cups) almond or coconut milk (see tip)
1 tablespoon mesquite powder
1 teaspoon rice malt syrup

Strawberry chia

40 g (1½ oz/¼ cup) chia seeds
250 ml (9 fl oz/1 cup) almond milk (see tip)
225 g (8 oz/1½ cups) strawberries,

I love a good porridge. This quinoa porridge is true soul food — deliciously comforting, and full of healthy ingredients, it's my family's go-to winter warmer.

Quinoa is gluten free, high in protein and fibre, and is low GI, meaning it is slowly digested for longer-lasting energy. Lucuma gives the porridge a natural sweet kick, with cinnamon and nutmeg for a touch of spice. Put it all together and you'll be powering on for hours.

Creamy quinoa porridge with stewed plums

SERVES 4 ⊗ VGN + DF + GF + RSF + NF

To stew the plums, place the ingredients in a saucepan with 125 ml (4 fl oz/½ cup) water. Bring to the boil, then reduce the heat and simmer for 5–8 minutes, or until the plums have softened slightly.

Remove the plums from the syrup. Continue simmering the syrup until it has reduced to a thick, sticky liquid; this can take up to 10 minutes. Remove the syrup from the heat and allow to cool. As it cools down, the syrup will thicken even further.

Meanwhile, make the porridge. Bring the quinoa and rice milk to the boil in a separate saucepan. Add the remaining porridge ingredients, stirring well. Bring to a simmer and cook for 3–5 minutes, stirring occasionally.

When your porridge has reached a thick, creamy consistency, remove from the heat and ladle into four serving bowls.

Serve warm, with the stewed plums and their syrup, and an extra drizzle of maple syrup.

TIP If you don't have any leftover cooked quinoa, you'll need to cook about 150 g (5½ oz/¾ cup) quinoa for this recipe. Place it in a small saucepan with 310 ml (10¾ fl oz/ 1¼ cups) water and bring to the boil. Reduce the heat, then cover and simmer for 10 minutes, or until tender. Cooked quinoa will keep in an airtight container in the fridge for 2–3 days.

Stewed plums
4 plums, cut in half, stones removed
2 tablespoons rice malt syrup
1 tablespoon granulated coconut sugar

Porridge
400 g (14 oz/2 cups) cooked quinoa (see tip)
375 ml (13 fl oz/1½ cups) rice milk
250 ml (9 fl oz/1 cup) coconut cream
2 tablespoons maple syrup, plus extra to serve
1 teaspoon lucuma powder
1 teaspoon ground cinnamon
½ teaspoon ground nutmeg
⅛ teaspoon Himalayan salt
2 tablespoons sunflower seeds
2 tablespoons chia seeds
1 tablespoon sultanas (golden raisins)

A raw version of the beloved breakfast granola, my RAWnola is based on one of my favourite gluten-free superfoods, the humble buckwheat seed, making these irresistible clusters high in protein, vitamin B, zinc, magnesium and antioxidants.

Dehydrating the RAWnola mixture is not essential, but is recommended if you'd like a crunchier result and an extended shelf life.

Once you've made yourself a batch, you'll find yourself snacking on it all day long.

RAWnola

SERVES 4 ✪ R + VGN + DF + GF + RSF

Place the dates, coconut oil and peanut butter in a food processor and pulse into a paste.

In a large bowl, combine the remaining ingredients. Add the date paste and use both hands (wearing some food-handling gloves, if you have some handy) to thoroughly combine all the ingredients, so the mixture sticks together.

If you have a food dehydrator, press the mixture onto a dehydrator tray, to about 5 mm (¼ inch) thick, and dehydrate at 40°C (105°F) for 8 hours. Once set, break the mixture into bite-sized pieces and store in an airtight container in the pantry. It will keep for up to 4 weeks.

If you don't have a food dehydrator, line a flat plate or tray with baking paper and spread the mixture on it, about 5 mm (¼ inch) thick. Set in the fridge for at least 2–3 hours. When your mixture is firm, your RAWnola is ready to eat. It will keep in an airtight container in the fridge for up to 3–5 days.

10 medjool dates, pitted
1 teaspoon coconut oil
1 tablespoon peanut butter
180 g (6 oz/1 cup) buckwheat groats
65 g (2¼ oz/¾ cup) desiccated coconut
1 tablespoon linseeds (flaxseeds)
1 teaspoon ground cinnamon
½ teaspoon maca powder

Baked beans and avocado on toast. When I think of a savoury breakfast, this is exactly what I go for.

The baked beans recipe is based on my mother's, and when we come home from a holiday abroad, we often gather around a traditional one-pot meal like this one.

For a feel-good meal the whole family will enjoy, serve on gluten-free seeded bread with heart-friendly avocado.

Baked beans & avocado on seeded loaf

SERVES 4 ✪ VGN + DF + GF + RSF

For the baked beans

Drain and rinse the beans; set aside.

Heat the oil in a large heavy-based saucepan. Add the onion and stir over medium heat for 2–3 minutes, or until the onion is translucent. Add the garlic and stir until fragrant. Stir the beans through until well combined.

Combine the tomato paste with the tinned tomatoes and 250 ml (9 fl oz/1 cup) water. Pour the mixture over the beans. Stir in the oregano, salt and pepper.

Bring to the boil, then reduce the heat, cover and simmer for 30–45 minutes, stirring every 10 minutes or so.

Remove the lid. Stir in an extra 125–250 ml (4–9 fl oz/½–1 cup) water, then cook, uncovered, for a further 10–20 minutes, or until the beans are tender.

For convenience, the beans can be cooked a few days ahead and stored in the fridge in an airtight container until required; reheat gently to serve.

For the loaf

Preheat the oven to 170°C (325°F).

Put the almond meal, psyllium husks, tapioca flour, bicarbonate of soda and salt in a bowl. Stir in 40 g (1½ oz/¼ cup) of the linseed meal.

Put the remaining linseed meal in a small bowl. Add 250 ml (9 fl oz/1 cup) water and whisk vigorously with a fork, then add to the almond meal mixture with the oil and mix until well combined. The batter should become dough-like.

Fold half the sunflower and chia seeds through. Pour the batter into a loaf (bar) tin, measuring about 24 x 13 cm (9½ x 5 inches), and about 6 cm (2½ inches) deep.

Sprinkle with the remaining sunflower and chia seeds and bake for about 30 minutes, or until the loaf is cooked through, and golden on top.

Remove from the oven and leave to cool before slicing. The bread will keep in an airtight container, at room temperature, for up to 2 days.

To serve

Toast the bread if desired and place a slice on each plate. Top with chunks of avocado and the warm beans. Serve immediately.

1 avocado, roughly chopped

Baked beans
380 g (13½ oz/2 cups) dried butterbeans, soaked in water overnight
2 tablespoons grapeseed oil
1 onion, finely diced
3 garlic cloves, crushed
1 heaped tablespoon tomato paste (concentrated purée)
400 g (14 oz) tin chopped tomatoes
1 tablespoon oregano leaves
½ teaspoon Himalayan salt, or to taste
⅛ teaspoon freshly ground black pepper

Gluten-free seeded loaf
300 g (10½ oz/3 cups) almond meal
40 g (1½ oz/½ cup) psyllium husks
60 g (2¼ oz/½ cup) tapioca flour
1 teaspoon bicarbonate of soda (baking soda)
¼ teaspoon Himalayan salt
300 g (10½ oz/2 cups) linseed (flaxseed) meal
60 ml (2 fl oz/¼ cup) grapeseed oil
40 g (1½ oz/¼ cup) sunflower seeds
40 g (1½ oz/¼ cup) chia seeds

We all love a piece of freshly baked banana bread, especially one that's sugar, gluten and wheat free. In our home, this banana and maple bread — made with a combination of nuts, seeds, fruit and gluten-free millet — is usually all eaten within a day or two. It is a perfect accompaniment to tea or coffee, or just on its own for a morning or afternoon snack.

Banana & maple bread

SERVES 8 ✖ VGN + DF + GF + RSF

Preheat the oven to 160°C (315°F). Line a loaf (bar) tin, measuring about 24 x 13 cm (9½ x 5 inches), and about 6 cm (2½ inches) deep, with baking paper.

Put the linseed meal in a bowl, mix in 185 ml (6 fl oz/¾ cup) water and place in the fridge for 5–10 minutes, or until the mixture gels together and takes on an egg-white consistency.

In a large bowl, combine the almond meal, coconut, millet flakes, cinnamon, vanilla, salt and bicarbonate of soda.

In a small bowl, mash two of the bananas using a fork. Mix in the coconut oil and maple syrup.

Add the banana mixture to the bowl of dry ingredients and mix until combined, then pour the batter into the loaf tin.

Slice the remaining banana and arrange over the loaf. Bake for 35–45 minutes, or until a skewer inserted into the middle of the loaf comes out clean.

Remove from the oven and leave to cool before slicing.

The loaf will keep for 2–3 days, stored in an airtight container in the fridge or at room temperature.

TIP For best results, use a clean coffee grinder to grind your own linseeds (flaxseeds) into a meal. In this recipe the linseed meal acts as an egg replacement and, when freshly ground, binds better than linseed meal that you buy already pre-ground.

40 g (1½ oz/¼ cup) plus 2 tablespoons linseed (flaxseed) meal

200 g (7 oz/2 cups) almond meal

45 g (1½ oz/½ cup) desiccated coconut

50 g (1¾ oz/½ cup) millet flakes

1 teaspoon ground cinnamon

1 teaspoon vanilla powder

⅛ teaspoon Himalayan salt

2 teaspoons bicarbonate of soda (baking soda)

3 ripe bananas

60 ml (2 fl oz/¼ cup) melted coconut oil

125 ml (4 fl oz/½ cup) maple syrup

Feel-good
detox juice *41*

×

Vegie brunch
board *40*

Nothing beats a lazy weekend brunch. It's the perfect late breakfast/early lunch situation for all of us who like a weekend sleep-in — who doesn't? — and also opens up a wider range of enticing meal offerings.

If you brunch with me, you'll be experiencing a colourful explosion of oven-baked vegies, scattered with spicy crumbed tofu pieces (our children's favourite). Add some seasoned avocado, grilled asparagus and crispy kale chips and you've got yourself some serious brunch biz.

Vegie brunch board

SERVES 2 ✕ VGN + DF + GF + RSF

Preheat the oven to 170°C (325°F). Line two baking trays with baking paper.

Start by crumbing the tofu. In a bowl, combine the almond meal, quinoa flakes, and nutritional yeast, then stir all the spices through. Pour the tamari into a small shallow bowl. Dip the tofu into the tamari, then coat with the seasoned almond meal mixture and place on one of the baking trays. Transfer to the oven and bake for 30–40 minutes, or until golden, turning the tofu over halfway during cooking. Keep warm.

While the tofu is in the oven, spread the pumpkin wedges on the other baking tray. Drizzle with the coconut oil, sprinkle with the rosemary leaves and bake for 25–30 minutes, or until cooked through, adding the tomatoes to the baking tray for the final 15 minutes, or until cooked to your liking.

When you're nearly ready to serve, heat a chargrill pan over medium heat. Lightly coat the asparagus spears with the grapeseed oil, season with salt and pepper and grill for 2–3 minutes, or until cooked to your desired tenderness.

To prepare the avocado, cut it into quarters and remove the stone and peel. Sprinkle with the lemon juice, olive oil, sunflower seeds and pepitas.

Arrange the warm pumpkin, tomatoes, asparagus, kale chips, avocado and baked tofu on a serving board or platter and serve.

½ butternut pumpkin, cut into wedges, seeds removed

1–2 teaspoons melted coconut oil

1 tablespoon roughly chopped rosemary leaves

2 truss tomatoes, halved

250 g (9 oz) asparagus spears, trimmed

1 teaspoon grapeseed oil

½ quantity Crispy kale chips (page 144), to serve

Spicy crumbed tofu

200 g (7 oz) medium-firm tofu, cut into squares or nuggets

2 tablespoons almond meal

1 tablespoon quinoa flakes

1 tablespoon nutritional yeast

¼ teaspoon dried parsley flakes

¼ teaspoon garlic powder

¼ teaspoon onion powder

⅛ teaspoon hot paprika

¼ teaspoon Himalayan salt, or to taste

⅛ teaspoon freshly ground black pepper

2 tablespoons gluten-free tamari

Seasoned avocado

1 avocado

1 teaspoon lemon juice

1 teaspoon olive oil

1 teaspoon sunflower seeds

1 tablespoon pepitas (pumpkin seeds)

*I'm not one of those healthies that goes on juice detoxes —
simply because I can't imagine not eating for days on end.
With the exception of my Choc peanut butter smoothie
bowl (page 45), I'd rather chew than slurp any day —
although this juice could almost persuade me otherwise!*

*It's perfectly sweet, totally delicious and bursting with
health benefits. Hot health terms such as 'cleansing',
'detoxifying', 'energising' and 'immune-boosting' all fit
into the mix when describing this one. Gotta love that.*

Feel-good detox juice

SERVES 1 ⊗ R + VGN + DF + GF + RSF + NF

1 medium-sized beetroot (beet), scrubbed well
1–2 carrots
1 small apple, cored and chopped
80 g (2¾ oz/½ cup) chopped pineapple
juice of ½ lemon
14 mint leaves
1–2 cm (½ inch) knob of fresh ginger

Mix all the ingredients in a juicer or blender and serve.

If you use a blender for this recipe, rather than a juicer,
you will get a much thicker (and more nutritious) juice, due
to the fibrous pulp from the fruit and veg being retained.
You can add a little water to the recipe to thin it, or run
the juice through a fine mesh sieve once it's blended.

It's great to have a go-to granola recipe to call on. There's just something about granola: the smell, the crunch, the taste, the comfort... my only problem is that I have no self-control when it's fresh out of the oven. Especially this ginger-spiced one, which is easy to make, utterly delicious and super healthy. I love to sprinkle it on almost anything. My husband often finds me in the pantry, munching on some straight from the jar! Serve with coconut yoghurt for a simple and satisfying breakfast.

Spiced ginger, pecan & pear granola

SERVES 4 ✖ VGN + DF + GF + RSF

Preheat the oven to 170°C (325°F).

Place the dates, maple syrup, coconut oil and orange juice in a food processor and blend until smooth.

In a large bowl, combine the oats, ginger, cinnamon, vanilla and salt. Add the date mixture and mix together well, until the oats are well coated and glossy.

Transfer the mixture to a baking tray, spreading it out evenly. Bake for 15–20 minutes, keeping an eye on it so it doesn't burn.

Add the coconut, pepitas, pecans and pears, tossing the mixture to ensure it toasts evenly. Bake for a further 15–20 minutes, or until the granola has browned, tossing once or twice if needed.

Remove from the oven and leave to cool for at least 20–30 minutes.

Store in an airtight container in the pantry. The granola will keep for up to 2 weeks.

5 medjool dates, pitted

125 ml (4 fl oz/½ cup) maple syrup

2 tablespoons coconut oil

60 ml (2 fl oz/¼ cup) orange juice

180 g (6 oz/2 cups) gluten-free rolled (porridge) oats

1 teaspoon ground ginger

1 tablespoon ground cinnamon

1 teaspoon vanilla powder

⅛ teaspoon Himalayan salt

35 g (1¼ oz/½ cup) shredded coconut

40 g (1½ oz/¼ cup) pepitas (pumpkin seeds)

25 g (1 oz/¼ cup) pecans

6 dried pears, left whole or roughly chopped

This must be my all-time favourite smoothie. The ultimate dessert for breakfast, it tastes so sinful you'll hardly believe it's good for you — with power foods like banana and raw cacao powder, and protein from the peanut butter. So easy to make (and too delicious not to remake!) it's a 'must try' for peanut-butter lovers.

Choc peanut butter smoothie bowl

SERVES 2 ⊗ R + VGN + DF + GF + RSF

2 frozen bananas, chopped, plus 1 fresh banana
1 tablespoon peanut butter, plus extra to serve
250 ml (9 fl oz/1 cup) coconut milk
250 ml (9 fl oz/1 cup) rice milk
1–2 tablespoons raw cacao powder, plus extra
   for sprinkling
½ teaspoon maca powder
1 teaspoon mesquite powder (optional)
2 tablespoons activated buckwheat groats

Place the frozen bananas in a blender. Add the peanut butter, coconut milk and rice milk, along with the cacao powder, maca and mesquite, if using. Whiz until smooth, then pour into two small bowls.

Slice the remaining banana and arrange over each bowl. Top with an extra dollop of peanut butter, then sprinkle with the buckwheat groats and extra cacao powder.

Devour!

I am so excited to share this recipe with you! These crunchy, chocolatey clusters take me back to the days when I used to eat crunchy chocolate-flavoured cereals daily. I'd almost forgotten how much I missed the taste until I came up with this recipe. Buckwheat and puffed quinoa give the perfect crunchy texture, while the tahini, cacao and coconut flavours combine effortlessly.

These crispy clusters make a fabulous topping to smoothie bowls, and are divine as a cereal with non-dairy milk.

Crunchy cacao & macadamia clusters

SERVES 6 ✕ VGN + DF + GF + RSF

Preheat the oven to 120°C (235°F). Line a 40 x 28 cm (16 x 11 inch) baking tray with baking paper.

Place the dates, maple syrup, coconut oil and tahini in a food processor and blend until smooth.

In a large bowl, combine the buckwheat groats, puffed quinoa, coconut, cacao powder and salt.

Things are going to get sticky, so you may want to pop on some food-handling gloves here. Add the date mixture to the buckwheat mixture and combine well using your hands. You want the mixture to stick together, so combine it all until it forms one large ball.

Place on the baking tray and spread the mixture out so it can bake evenly. Drizzle with the grapeseed oil.

Bake for 15–20 minutes, then loosely break up the mixture into clusters, shaking the tray or tossing to ensure they brown evenly. Bake for a further 15–20 minutes, or until the clusters have browned and become crispy.

Remove from the oven and leave to cool for at least 20–30 minutes. The clusters should become crunchy once cooled.

Add the macadamias and store in an airtight container in the pantry. The clusters will keep for up to 2 weeks.

TIP For a nut-free version, replace the macadamias with your favourite seeds, or mix of seeds.

10 medjool dates, pitted

60 ml (2 fl oz/¼ cup) maple syrup

2 tablespoons coconut oil

1 tablespoon tahini

280 g (10 oz/1½ cups) activated buckwheat groats

60 g (2¼ oz/1½ cups) puffed quinoa

90 g (3¼ oz/1 cup) desiccated coconut

85 g (3 oz/¾ cup) raw cacao powder

⅛ teaspoon Himalayan salt

1 tablespoon grapeseed oil

60 g (2¼ oz/½ cup) roughly chopped macadamia nuts (see tip)

There are so many muesli options out there — my local health food store has a whole aisle dedicated to them. I haven't found a combination from the store that I really love, so I've made my own. To me, the flavour combination of buckwheat, coconut, strawberries, nuts and seeds is just divine, and the balance of crunch and chew spot on.

I sprinkle it on our smoothies, overnight oats (page 26), quinoa porridge (page 30) and chia puddings (page 28), or simply enjoy a bowl with rice milk, instead of cereal.

Raw breakfast sprinkles

SERVES 4 ✪ R + VGN + DF + GF + RSF

180 g (6 oz/1 cup) activated buckwheat groats
30 g (1 oz/½ cup) coconut flakes
70 g (2½ oz/½ cup) dried white mulberries
25 g (1 oz/½ cup) freeze-dried strawberries
40 g (1½ oz/¼ cup) roughly chopped Brazil nuts
40 g (1½ oz/¼ cup) chia seeds
1 tablespoon sunflower seeds

Combine all the ingredients in a bowl and store in an airtight jar in the pantry.

The sprinkles will keep for up to 2 weeks.

Sticky coconut rice: the stuff of tropical island dreams. My dad often made rice pudding for us, and I vividly remember the heavenly aroma of the cinnamon and cloves cooking with the milk. My version uses coconut milk and Thai sticky purple rice, which you'll find at good health food stores and Asian grocers. Pair it with caramelised banana for a taste of tropical paradise.

Sticky coconut rice with caramelised banana

SERVES 2 ✗ VGN + DF + GF + RSF + NF

Place the rice, cloves and cinnamon stick in a saucepan. Stir in 250 ml (9 fl oz/1 cup) water and bring to the boil, then reduce the heat to low. Cover and simmer for 15–20 minutes, or until the water has been absorbed.

Stir in the coconut milk and bring back to the boil, then reduce the heat to a simmer. Stir in the rice malt syrup and cook, uncovered, for 30 minutes, stirring frequently.

Remove the cloves and cinnamon stick and cook, stirring, for a further 30 minutes, or until the rice is sticky and the liquid has been well absorbed.

Near serving time, preheat the oven to 180°C (350°F). Spread the coconut on a baking tray lined with baking paper and toast in the oven for 7–8 minutes, or until light golden brown, shaking the tray once or twice to ensure even baking. Remove from the oven to cool.

To caramelise the banana, heat the coconut oil in a small frying pan over medium–high heat. Add the banana and cinnamon. Cook, turning occasionally, for 5 minutes, or until the banana is lightly browned on each side.

Spoon the sticky rice into serving bowls. Top with the caramelised banana and coconut flakes, and a drizzle of extra rice malt syrup. Serve warm.

This dish can also be enjoyed cold; the rice will keep in an airtight container in the fridge for 2–3 days.

100 g (3½ oz/½ cup) Thai sticky purple rice
3–4 cloves
1 cinnamon stick
1 litre (35 fl oz/4 cups) coconut milk
125–250 ml (4–9 fl oz/½–1 cup) rice malt syrup, or to taste, plus extra to serve
15 g (½ oz/¼ cup) coconut flakes

Caramelised banana
1 teaspoon coconut oil
1 banana, sliced lengthways
½ teaspoon ground cinnamon

Anyone who knew me when I was growing up knew about my serious addiction to choc hazelnut spread, which I'd eat straight out of the jar, several times a day. These days I get my fix with this divine superfood version. Deliciously smooth, it is loved by my whole family, so I get to carry on my childhood tradition with my own children, without the nasties. Happy kids and happy mama!

Choc hazelnut spread

SERVES 12 ✖ VGN + DF + GF + RSF

270 g (9½ oz/2 cups) hazelnuts
1 teaspoon vanilla extract
25 g (1 oz/¼ cup) raw cacao powder
pinch of Himalayan salt
125 ml (4 fl oz/½ cup) rice malt syrup
1 tablespoon coconut oil
185 ml (6 fl oz/¾ cup) non-dairy milk of your choice

Preheat the oven to 160ºC (315ºF).

Spread the hazelnuts on a baking tray and bake for 5–10 minutes, or until browned. Remove from the oven and leave to cool slightly, then rub off the skins.

Place the hazelnuts in a high-speed food processor. Blend for 2–3 minutes, or until they turn into a butter. Add all the remaining ingredients and process until smooth.

Store in an airtight container in the fridge. It will keep for up to 2 weeks, and is especially delicious with the Gluten-free seeded loaf on page 34.

Chia has to be God's gift to healthy breakfast lovers. It is seriously the easiest, most practical and addictive brekkie option around. Here I've paired a vanilla chia with a lovely berry cream and matcha-flavoured cashew swirl, for real wow factor. This recipe is simple to pull together, but the setting time for the chia and cashew components is lengthy, so you may want to prepare those bits ahead.

Vanilla chia with berry cashew cream & matcha swirl

SERVES 2 ⊗ R + VGN + DF + GF + RSF

Place the chia seeds in a bowl with the rice milk and coconut yoghurt and mix well with a fork. Add the vanilla powder and rice malt syrup and mix again.

Set in the fridge for at least 2–3 hours, or overnight.

To make the cashew cream, drain the cashews and place in a food processor. Add the coconut oil, coconut milk, rice malt syrup and vanilla and blend until the nuts are broken down and the filling is smooth.

Pour half the cashew cream into a cup or bowl and set aside.

Add the berry cream ingredients to the cashew cream in the processor and whiz until smooth. Pour into two serving glasses and set in the fridge for 2–3 hours.

To make the matcha swirl, simply mix the matcha powder into the reserved cashew cream. Set in the freezer for 2–3 hours. The actual

setting time is just approximate. You are going to pipe the mixture into swirls, so it needs to be firm enough to hold its shape, but not too hard to squeeze through the piping (icing) tube.

When ready to serve, spoon the soaked chia seeds into your serving glasses, over the blueberry cream. Sprinkle with the buckwheat groats.

Place the matcha mixture in a piping (icing) bag fitted with a star nozzle. Applying pressure to the top of the bag, pipe in a steady movement around the edge of the glass, building up into a swirl. When you reach the end of the swirl press down slightly, release the pressure and pull the nozzle up quickly. If you find the matcha mixture is too firm to pipe, leave it at room temperature to soften slightly, but keep an eye on it, as it can soften fairly quickly.

Sprinkle with blueberry powder, if desired, and enjoy straightaway.

40 g (1½ oz/¼ cup) chia seeds
250 ml (9 fl oz/1 cup) rice milk
140 g (5 oz/½ cup) coconut yoghurt, or other non-dairy yoghurt
1 teaspoon vanilla powder
1–2 teaspoons rice malt syrup or maple syrup (optional)
1 tablespoon activated buckwheat groats
blueberry powder, for sprinkling (optional)

Cashew cream
150 g (5½ oz/1 cup) cashews, soaked for at least 4 hours
60 ml (2 fl oz/¼ cup) coconut oil
125 ml (4½ fl oz/½ cup) coconut milk or almond milk
80 ml (2½ fl oz/⅓ cup) rice malt syrup
½ teaspoon vanilla powder

Berry cream
1–2 teaspoons blueberry powder, or a handful of fresh or frozen blueberries

Matcha swirl
1 teaspoon matcha (green tea) powder

Fruit platter with
orange lime dressing &
strawberry yoghurt *62*

×

Carrot cake muffins *59*

THE WEEKEND SPREAD

Breakfast for that lazy Sunday

Buckwheat pancakes with
raw chocolate sauce *58*

×

Oat waffles with blueberry
lavender cream *63*

Every Sunday, my dad made us pancakes with chocolate spread for breakfast. I remember the smell, the taste and the general feel-good vibes that followed.

I like to continue the tradition with my own kids, so we have these buckwheat pancakes most weekends and smother them with a wickedly delightful raw chocolate sauce. Taste sensation! Just don't blame me for your new-found addiction...

Buckwheat pancakes with raw chocolate sauce

SERVES 4 ⊗ VGN + DF + GF + RSF + NF

To make the pancakes, combine the buckwheat flour, potato flour, coconut flour, baking powder and salt in a large bowl.

Add the coconut milk, coconut oil and 125 ml (4 fl oz/½ cup) water and whisk well. The amount of water you need depends on how thick you prefer your batter; I like mine fairly thin, so I add a bit more — usually another 125 ml (4 fl oz/½ cup) water.

Heat a non-stick frying pan over medium heat. Brush the pan with some of the grapeseed oil.

Pour 60 ml (2 fl oz/¼ cup) of the batter into the pan and cook for 2–3 minutes, or until bubbles appear on the surface. Turn and cook the other side for 2 minutes, or until cooked through. Transfer to a plate and keep warm.

Cook the remaining batter in the same way, adding more grapeseed oil to the pan as needed. You should have enough batter to make eight pancakes.

Meanwhile, make the raw chocolate sauce. Whisk the coconut oil, maple syrup and cacao powder together in a bowl, then whisk in the vanilla powder and tahini until smooth.

Divide the warm pancakes among serving plates, along with the bananas. Drizzle with the chocolate sauce and tuck straight in.

2 bananas, peeled and cut in half lengthways

Buckwheat pancakes
130 g (4½ oz/1 cup) buckwheat flour
2 tablespoons potato flour or ground yellow maize flour
2 tablespoons coconut flour
2 teaspoons gluten-free baking powder
⅛ teaspoon Himalayan salt
375 ml (13 fl oz/1½ cups) coconut milk or other non-dairy milk
1 tablespoon melted coconut oil
1–2 teaspoons grapeseed oil

Raw chocolate sauce
125 ml (4 fl oz/½ cup) melted coconut oil
60 ml (2 fl oz/¼ cup) maple syrup
85 g (3 oz/¾ cup) raw cacao powder
1 teaspoon vanilla powder (optional)
2 tablespoons tahini

I adore carrots in baking. There's something irresistible about the gorgeous smell that escapes from the oven when carrots are combined with spices. These muffins are easy to whip up, and totally nutritious. Slather them with my lemon cashew whip and you'll have a new favourite weekend breakfast ritual.

Carrot cake muffins

MAKES 6 ✪ VGN + DF + GF + RSF

Preheat the oven to 170°C (325°F). Line a six-hole giant (250 ml/9 fl oz/ 1 cup) muffin tin with paper cases.

Put the linseed meal in a bowl, mix in 125 ml (4 fl oz/½ cup) water and place in the fridge for 5–10 minutes, or until the mixture gels together and takes on an egg-white consistency.

In a large bowl, combine the almond meal, buckwheat flour, cinnamon, nutmeg, salt and bicarbonate of soda.

In a separate bowl, combine the coconut oil, rice malt syrup, apple sauce and milk.

Add the wet ingredients to the dry ingredients, along with the linseed mixture, and mix together until only just combined. Stir the carrot, walnuts and sultanas through.

Pour the batter into the muffin paper cases. Sprinkle with the coconut sugar, if desired, and bake for 35–45 minutes, or until a skewer

inserted into the middle of a muffin comes out clean.

Remove from the oven and leave to cool completely before icing.

To make the lemon cashew whip, blend the milk, rice malt syrup and coconut oil in a high-speed blender. Add the cashews and whiz until smooth. Add the vanilla, salt and lemon juice and blend until smooth.

Using a piping (icing) bag, swirl the cashew whip over the muffins. Sprinkle with a dusting of cinnamon.

The muffins will keep in an airtight container in the fridge for 1–2 days.

TIP *For best results, use a clean coffee grinder to grind your own linseeds (flaxseeds) into a meal. In this recipe the linseed meal acts as an egg replacement and, when freshly ground, binds better than linseed meal that you buy already pre-ground.*

50 g (1¾ oz/⅓ cup) linseed (flaxseed) meal (see tip)
150 g (5½ oz/1½ cups) almond meal
200 g (7 oz/1½ cups) buckwheat flour
1 tablespoon ground cinnamon
1 teaspoon ground nutmeg
⅛ teaspoon Himalayan salt
1½ teaspoons bicarbonate of soda (baking soda)
125 ml (4 fl oz/½ cup) melted coconut oil
250 ml (9 fl oz/1 cup) rice malt syrup
135 g (4¾ oz/½ cup) unsweetened apple sauce
125 ml (4 fl oz/½ cup) non-dairy milk of your choice
310 g (1½ oz/2 cups) grated carrot
30 g (1 oz/¼ cup) walnuts, chopped
45 g (1½ oz/¼ cup) sultanas (golden raisins)
1 tablespoon granulated coconut sugar (optional)

Lemon cashew whip
60 ml (2 fl oz/¼ cup) non-dairy milk of your choice
60 ml (2 fl oz/¼ cup) rice malt syrup
2 tablespoons coconut oil
150 g (5½ oz/1 cup) cashews, soaked for 1 hour
1 teaspoon natural vanilla extract
pinch of Himalayan salt
2 teaspoons lemon juice
ground cinnamon, for dusting

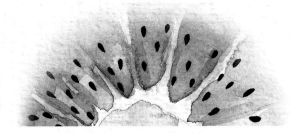

IT'S NOT A DIET,
IT'S A LIFESTYLE

Fruit has to be the most wonderful food to eat, plate and photograph. My hungry kiddies and I love to eat a fruit arrangement just as much as I relish playing around with colours, cutting styles and flavour combinations. Fruit platters satisfy our sweet tooth, while also providing energy and plenty of vitamins and minerals to set us up for a productive day.

Fruit platter with orange lime dressing & strawberry yoghurt

SERVES 2 ✖ R + VGN + DF + GF + RSF + NF

Cut the pineapple, dragonfruit, mango and kiwi fruit decoratively, and chop the passionfruit into quarters. Arrange on a platter with the strawberries, then scatter the blueberries and pomegranate seeds around. Drizzle the fruit with the pulp from one or two of the passionfruit quarters.

Combine the orange lime dressing ingredients and drizzle over the fruit.

To make the strawberry yoghurt, blend the strawberries, lime juice, vanilla and rice malt syrup in a blender until the mixture forms a purée.

Fold the strawberry purée through the coconut yoghurt and serve with the fruit platter.

TIP *To make your own coconut yoghurt, chill 400 g (14 oz) full-fat coconut cream in the fridge for 4–5 hours. Place in a bowl with ½ teaspoon non-dairy yoghurt culture or starter culture, add 1 tablespoon tapioca starch and mix together well. Pour into a sterilised 500 ml (17 fl oz/2 cup) glass jar and seal the lid. Turn your oven light on and pop the jar into the oven to incubate for 12 hours — you don't actually want the oven on, just the light. Transfer the yoghurt to your fridge for at least 8 hours before consuming. It will keep in the fridge for 2–3 days.*

1 pineapple slice, skin removed
½ dragonfruit
1 mango
2 kiwi fruit
2 passionfruit
8 strawberries, halved
75 g (2½ oz/½ cup) blueberries
1 tablespoon pomegranate seeds

Orange lime dressing
1 tablespoon orange juice
1–2 teaspoons lime juice
pulp of 1 passionfruit
grated zest of ½ lime

Strawberry yoghurt
10 fresh strawberries
1 tablespoon lime juice
½ teaspoon vanilla powder
2 teaspoons rice malt syrup
280 g (10 oz/1 cup) plain unsweetened
    coconut yoghurt (to make your own,
    see tip)

Nothing beats a waffle Sunday — the smell of waffles cooking, tea brewing, the sight of fresh fruit on display, the precious family time together, and the excitement of knowing that it's your day. A free day where you choose what you want to do. And, of course, you choose waffles. These nutty oat waffles are the perfect start to your Sunday: a little slice of heaven on the best day of the week.

Oat waffles with blueberry lavender cream

MAKES 4–6 WAFFLES ✖ VGN + DF + GF + RSF

Start by making the blueberry cream. Drain and rinse the cashews, then place in a food processor with the rice malt syrup, coconut oil and coconut milk. Blend until smooth. Add the almond butter and pulse until well combined, then add the remaining ingredients and process until thick and creamy. Place in the fridge to set for 2–3 hours.

When ready to serve, place the 45 g (1½ oz/½ cup) oats in your food processor and reduce to fine crumbs. Tip into a bowl, add the buckwheat flour, linseed meal, almond meal, bicarbonate of soda and salt and mix until well combined.

Add 125 ml (4 fl oz/½ cup) water and your choice of milk and stir until well combined. Fold the extra tablespoon of oats through.

Turn on your waffle maker and brush with the coconut oil.

Spoon some batter into the waffle maker and leave for 2–5 minutes, or until cooked through. During cooking, keep an eye on the temperature — I often turn the waffle maker on and off so it doesn't get too hot and burn the waffles. The waffles should be firm on the outside, but perfectly moist when you take a bite.

Transfer to a plate and keep warm while cooking the remaining batter. You should end up with four to six waffles, depending on the size of your waffle maker.

Serve the waffles warm, topped with the blueberry cream and fresh blueberries, and a sprinkling of lavender if desired.

TIP *Make the blueberry cream the day before, to give it time to set to a lovely, thick consistency.*

45 g (1½ oz/½ cup) gluten-free rolled (porridge) oats, plus an extra 1 tablespoon
60 g (2¼ oz/½ cup) buckwheat flour (or teff flour)
2 tablespoons linseed (flaxseed) meal
2 tablespoons almond meal (or ground pepitas/pumpkin seeds for nut free)
1 tablespoon bicarbonate of soda (baking soda)
⅛ teaspoon Himalayan salt
375 ml (13 fl oz/1½ cups) rice milk, almond milk or coconut milk
1–2 teaspoons melted coconut oil
fresh blueberries, to serve
1–2 teaspoons finely chopped fresh organic lavender (optional)

Blueberry cream
150 g (5½ oz/1 cup) cashews, soaked overnight
125 ml (4½ fl oz/½ cup) rice malt syrup
60 ml (2 fl oz/¼ cup) coconut oil
60–125 ml (2–4½ fl oz/¼–½ cup) coconut milk
1 tablespoon almond butter
75 g (2½ oz/½ cup) blueberries
1 teaspoon vanilla powder
1 tablespoon lemon juice

I'm all for convenience. Let's face it, we live in a busy, fast-paced world in which adding more to our to-do list can be overkill. But this homemade almond milk is as simple and as natural as it gets, and tastes amazing! Add the simple flavour variations below and you may just leave those store-bought varieties behind for good.

Homemade almond, chocolate and coffee milks

SERVES 1 ✖ R + VGN + DF + GF + RSF

Drain and rinse the almonds. Place in a high-speed blender with the water and salt and whiz until smooth. This may take 3–4 minutes, depending on the strength of your blender.

Set a nut milk bag or straining bag over a bowl, then pour the almond milk through. You will notice the almond pulp in your nut milk bag or strainer. To get the most out of your milk, squeeze the bag firmly to force all the liquid to seep through. If using a strainer, place the pulp in a tea towel and firmly squeeze the tea towel over the bowl, to achieve the same effect. You should have about 750 ml (26 fl oz/3 cups) of almond milk in your bowl.

Nut milk is best served cold, so store your almond milk in a clean airtight jar in the fridge and consume within 24 hours.

To make the spiced chocolate milk, or the coffee milk, rinse out the blender and pour your 750 ml (26 fl oz/3 cups) freshly strained almond milk back in. Add the dates, then the remaining ingredients, and blend on high speed until smooth and creamy.

Pour the milk into a clean airtight jar and cool in the fridge for a few hours. It is best consumed within 24 hours.

160 g (5½ oz/1 cup) almonds, soaked for 8 hours
1 litre (35 fl oz/4 cups) filtered water
¼ teaspoon Himalayan salt

Spiced chocolate milk
4 medjool dates, pitted
2 heaped tablespoons raw cacao powder
¼ teaspoon ground cinnamon
¼ teaspoon ground nutmeg
⅛ teaspoon Himalayan salt

Coffee milk
4 medjool dates, pitted
100 ml (3½ fl oz) espresso coffee
1 tablespoon tahini
½ teaspoon vanilla powder
⅛ teaspoon Himalayan salt

From top: Homemade
almond milk
×
Coffee milk
×
Spiced chocolate milk

I'm obsessed with nut butters. As you've noticed, I use them in many of my recipes. I can go on and on about their amazing versatility and how creamy and delicious they are — they're such a great snack option, and perfect in all kinds of sweet and savoury dishes.

So, here are four simple recipes that will turn you into a nut butter pro. You'll be whipping up all kinds of nut butters in no time. Once you've created the basic versions here, you can combine other nuts to create more favourite combos.

Homemade nut butters

SERVES 12 ⊗ VGN + DF + GF + RSF

Peanut butter
550 g (1 lb 4 oz/4 cups) peanuts
½ teaspoon Himalayan salt

Almond butter
650 g (1 lb 7 oz/4 cups) almonds
½ teaspoon Himalayan salt

Cashew butter
625 g (1 lb 6 oz/4 cups) cashews
½ teaspoon Himalayan salt

Pistachio & macadamia butter
350 g (12 oz/2½ cups) pistachio nut
   kernels
230 g (8 oz/1½ cups) macadamia nuts
½ teaspoon Himalayan salt

If using raw nuts

Place your chosen nuts in a high-speed food processor. Add the salt, if desired, then start blending, stopping now and then to give the motor a rest, and to scrape down the sides of the processor bowl. The blending time will depend on how powerful your processor is, and how smooth and creamy you like your nut butter; it may take 20–30 minutes.

Store your nut butter in a clean jar in the fridge. It will keep for up to 3 weeks.

If toasting raw nuts

Preheat the oven to 150ºC (300ºF).

Line a baking tray with baking paper. Spread your chosen nuts on the baking tray, sprinkle with the salt and bake for 10–15 minutes, or until golden, shaking the tray occasionally to ensure they don't burn.

Transfer the toasted nuts to a high-speed food processor and start blending. The blending time will depend on how smooth and creamy you like your nut butter, and how powerful your processor is. It can take up to 10–20 minutes to achieve a smooth nut butter, and you'll need to stop and scrape down the sides of the processor bowl a few times, and to give the motor a rest. The nut butter is complete when it is smooth and creamy, with no nut pieces — unless you prefer a crunchy nut butter, in which case you can stop processing earlier.

Store your nut butter in a clean jar in the fridge. It will keep for up to 3 weeks.

If using soaked/activated raw nuts

In a large non-metallic bowl, combine the nuts and salt. Pour in enough water to cover the nuts and mix well to dissolve the salt. Cover with a plate or saucepan lid and leave in a warm place for 12 hours.

The next day, rinse the nuts and dry them with a tea towel. Preheat the oven to 150ºC (300ºF), or set up a food dehydrator.

Spread the nuts on a baking tray lined with baking paper, or on your food dehydrator trays. Bake in the oven, or dehydrate at 60ºC (140ºF), for 12–24 hours, shaking the baking tray occasionally if using the oven.

Allow to cool, then place the nuts in your food processor. The blending time will be longer than for toasted nuts, and can take 20–30 minutes, depending on how powerful your processor is, and how smooth and creamy you like your nut butter. You'll need to stop frequently to give the motor a rest, and to scrape down the sides of the processor bowl.

Store your nut butter in a clean jar in the fridge. It will keep for up to 3 weeks.

SMOOTHIE LOVE

Let's drink the rainbow

I wouldn't call myself the green smoothie type. Let's just say I prefer chocolate... but you knew that already.

This smooth combo tips that old theory on its head, and will turn you into one of those 'daily green smoothie' healthies. Yep, believe it — I can happily admit this is now my first choice when it comes to morning smoothie options.

For a sweeter option, add some pineapple and use just 125 ml (4 fl oz/½ cup) coconut water.

Super greens smoothie

SERVES 1 ✪ R + VGN + DF + GF + RSF + NF

50 g (1¾ oz/1 cup) mixed green vegie leaves,
   such as spinach, rocket (arugula) and kale
½ Lebanese (short) cucumber, roughly chopped
1 celery stalk, chopped
1 cm (½ inch) knob of fresh ginger
flesh of ¼ avocado
juice of 1 lime
a handful of green grapes
2 tablespoons coconut yoghurt
125–250 ml (4–9 fl oz/½–1 cup) coconut water
2 ice cubes

Place all the ingredients in a high-speed blender and whiz until smooth.

   Pour into your glass and enjoy straightaway.

Berries and cacao: full of antioxidants, this smoothie doesn't just taste the bomb, it is literally brimming with vitality, with seven health-giving superfoods delivering loads of nourishment in one quick hit. Yes, we love that! Whether for breakfast or an afternoon pick-me-up, this one's a winner.

Jam-packed with nutrition, this smoothie is a morning must. Containing avocado, spinach and chia seeds, it really is a powerhouse, and will provide all the energy you need to get going and power through your day. It's also great as a replenishing thirst-quencher after a workout. And it tastes amazing.

CocoBerry superfood smoothie

SERVES 1 ✕ R + VGN + DF + GF + RSF + NF

250 ml (9 fl oz/1 cup) non-dairy milk, such as rice, almond or coconut milk
125 g (4½ oz/1 cup) mixed frozen berries
1 frozen banana, chopped
flesh from ¼ avocado
2 medjool dates, pitted
1½ tablespoons raw cacao powder
1 teaspoon chia seeds (optional)

Add the milk to your blender, followed by the remaining ingredients. Blend on high for 30 seconds, or until the smoothie is creamy.

Pour into your serving glass and enjoy.

Blueberry powerhouse smoothie

SERVES 1 ✕ R + VGN + DF + GF + RSF + NF

125 ml (4½ fl oz/½ cup) coconut milk
125 ml (4½ fl oz/½ cup) rice milk
1 frozen banana, chopped
310 g (11 oz/2 cups) frozen blueberries
25 g (1 oz/½ cup) baby English spinach leaves
flesh of ½ avocado
1 teaspoon chia seeds (optional)

Add the coconut milk and rice milk to your blender, followed by the remaining ingredients.

Blend on high for 30 seconds, or until the smoothie is creamy — you may need to add a few more glugs of coconut milk or rice milk to get your blender going.

Pour into your serving glass and slurp it down.

This is my go-to smoothie when I'm feeling nostalgic for a summer trip abroad. It's the perfect combination of sweet and sour, with the most divine smell that will leave you hankering for somewhere tropical, or anywhere sun, sand and ocean are involved.

This one's for lovers. For the lovers who choose strawberry over chocolate and vanilla. The lovers who crave strawberry ice cream, but settle for this satisfying smoothie instead.

This one's for you. The smoothie you'll come back to over and over, and the one you will love me for. Usually I'd choose chocolate over anything, but this smoothie has me joining your strawberry lovers' club. It's that good.

Tropical smoothie

SERVES 1 ⊗ R + VGN + DF + GF + RSF + NF

125 ml (4½ fl oz/½ cup) coconut milk
125 ml (4½ fl oz/½ cup) rice milk
juice of ½ lime
1 frozen banana, chopped
flesh of 1 mango
1 slice pineapple, skin removed
pulp of 1 passionfruit
mint leaves, to garnish

Pour the coconut milk, rice milk and lime juice into your blender. Add the banana, mango, pineapple and passionfruit pulp.

Blend on high for 30 seconds, or until the smoothie is creamy. Pour into your serving glass, garnish with mint leaves and set sail for the tropics.

Strawberry lover's smoothie

SERVES 1 ⊗ R + VGN + DF + GF + RSF

125 ml (4½ fl oz/½ cup) coconut milk
125 ml (4½ fl oz/½ cup) rice milk
1 tablespoon coconut yoghurt
150 g (5½ oz/1 cup) frozen strawberries
   (if you use fresh strawberries, the smoothie
   won't be quite so lovely and thick)
1 large frozen banana, chopped
1 tablespoon almond butter
1 teaspoon chia seeds
½ teaspoon vanilla powder

Add the coconut milk, rice milk and coconut yoghurt to your blender, followed by the remaining ingredients.

Blend on high for 30 seconds, or until the smoothie is creamy. Pour into your serving glass and relish every sip.

From left: CocoBerry
superfood smoothie *70*

×

Strawberry lover's
smoothie *71*

×

Blueberry powerhouse
smoothie *70*

CAMILLE'S PICK

×

Tropical smoothie *71*

Smoothie time! Banana and cinnamon are a perfect match in this thick and creamy combo, which has just the right amount of sweetness and spice.

I've added tahini, firstly because I love it, secondly because it's a good source of calcium, and thirdly because it adds a beautiful nutty flavour.

There are so many reasons to try this one...

Banana cinnamon smoothie

SERVES 1 ⊗ R + VGN + DF + GF + RSF + NF

250 ml (9 fl oz/1 cup) coconut milk
125 ml (4½ fl oz/½ cup) rice milk
2 frozen bananas, chopped
1 tablespoon desiccated coconut
1 tablespoon tahini
1 teaspoon ground cinnamon (freshly ground is best)
1 teaspoon mesquite powder (optional)
1 medjool date, pitted (optional, if you're a sweet tooth!)

Add the coconut milk and rice milk to your blender, followed by the remaining ingredients.

Blend on high for 30 seconds, or until the smoothie is creamy. Pour into your serving glass and enjoy.

SEB'S PICK

Forget what you know about hot chocolate. Let me show you what I think real hot chocolate should taste like.

Made with coconut milk, real chocolate and the pure extract of mint leaves, there is no better way to truly enjoy the decadent duo of mint and chocolate than with this seductively rich and creamy stovetop hot chocolate.

This one is sure to blow your mind — in a good way, of course.

Creamy mint hot chocolate

SERVES 2 ✪ VGN + DF + GF + RSF

250 ml (9 fl oz/1 cup) coconut milk

125–250 ml (4–9 fl oz/½–1 cup) almond or rice milk, or other non-dairy milk

35 g (1¼ oz/¼ cup) chopped dark unsweetened chocolate

1 tablespoon raw cacao powder

1 tablespoon maple syrup

½ teaspoon lucuma powder (optional)

4–5 drops natural peppermint extract

⅛ teaspoon Himalayan salt

Place the coconut milk and other non-dairy milk in a saucepan over medium heat. Add the chocolate and stir until melted.

Stir in the remaining ingredients and bring to a gentle boil. Pour the hot chocolate into two serving cups and prepare to be amazed.

I have a real love affair with chai tea lattes. I love everything about these lush spicy warmers: the taste, the aroma, the comfort... heaven in a cup.

Many chai mixes are laden with sugar. To make your own, all you need are some whole spices, a chai craving and a spare 30 minutes or so for the flavours to steep.

Chai tea lattes

SERVES 2 ✪ VGN + DF + GF + RSF + NF

1 cm (½ inch) sliver of fresh ginger

1 cinnamon stick

5 cloves

3 cardamom pods

1 star anise

¼ of a whole nutmeg

1–2 organic black tea bags (or rooibos tea bags for a caffeine-free option)

250 ml (9 fl oz/1 cup) non-dairy milk, such as coconut or rice milk

1–2 teaspoons maple syrup

1 teaspoon ground cinnamon

Place all the spices in a saucepan. Pour in 500 ml (17 fl oz/2 cups) water and bring to the boil. Reduce the heat and simmer, uncovered, for up to 30 minutes; the longer you simmer, the more chai flavour you will get.

Add the tea bags and leave to steep for 2 minutes.

Meanwhile, heat your milk in a saucepan or using a milk frother.

Strain the tea through a fine-mesh sieve, discarding the tea bags and spices, then pour the tea into two mugs. Stir in maple syrup to taste.

Pour the warm milk into the mugs, sprinkle with the cinnamon, settle back and enjoy.

LUNCH
VIBES

I was a late convert to Mexican-inspired tastes. I thought cheese was a necessary component so I just didn't go there.

But I love beans and enjoy them in so many different contexts, so to meet my bean cravings I gave vegan tacos and burritos a go. I combined red kidney beans with an array of colourful fresh vegies and a beautiful avocado smash and realised what I'd been missing out on. The lime and chilli really bring out the best of these natural plant-based ingredients.

Deliciously appetising, and an easy crowd-pleasing meal, this is one you'll make over and over.

Vegie burrito

SERVES 4 ✕ VGN + DF + GF + RSF + NF

Heat the olive oil in a chargrill pan over medium–high heat. Add the corn cobs and chargrill for about 10 minutes, turning the cobs over so the kernels char evenly.

Remove the cobs from the pan and leave until cool enough to handle, then shave the kernels off the cob using a sharp knife. Set aside.

Lay the tortillas flat on a clean work surface. Arrange the beans, carrot, cabbage, onion and capsicum on top of each one.

Scoop the avocado flesh into a shallow bowl. Add the salt and lime juice and roughly smash using a fork — you want the avocado to soften, yet still be a little chunky.

Place the corn and a generous spoonful of avocado smash over each tortilla.

Combine all the dressing ingredients in a small bowl, then drizzle over each tortilla.

Sprinkle with your choice of herbs, then fold up and serve immediately.

1 tablespoon olive oil

2 corn cobs

4 gluten-free corn tortillas

350 g (12 oz/2 cups) cooked or tinned red kidney beans, rinsed and drained

2 carrots, grated

½ purple cabbage, shredded

1 red onion, diced

1 red capsicum (pepper), diced

2 ripe avocados

¼ teaspoon Himalayan salt, or to taste

juice of 1 lime

chopped coriander (cilantro) and/or snipped chives, to garnish

Dressing

2 tablespoons extra virgin olive oil

1 red chilli, chopped

1 garlic clove, crushed

juice of 1 lime

⅛ teaspoon Himalayan salt, or to taste

⅛ teaspoon freshly cracked black pepper

I don't know what I was eating before I discovered rice paper rolls. Now I'm obsessed! There are many variations out there, but with its array of crispy colourful vegetables, tofu and a magic dipping sauce, I think this one's pretty special — a vegetarian's dream, and a party favourite.

Make these for your next event and you'll have a hard time trying not to gobble them up yourself before the party even gets started.

Rainbow summer rolls

MAKES 10 ⊗ R + VGN + DF + GF + RSF

Cut the tofu, beetroot, carrots, cucumber and capsicums into long thin strips, keeping them separate. Have the cabbage, basil and micro herbs nearby. Cut the avocado in half, remove the stone and peel, then cut each half into five slices.

Fill a bowl with lukewarm water. Submerge one rice paper sheet into the water for about 15 seconds, or until the sheet is just soft; don't leave it in too long or it will become soggy and tear very easily. Place on a clean tea towel or paper towel.

Arrange a small portion of the assorted vegetables, tofu, a slice of avocado, two basil leaves and some micro herbs along the centre of the rice paper round, leaving about 5 cm (2 inches) of wrapper uncovered on each side. I like to arrange the different ingredients in colour order, to get a rainbow effect, but this is not essential. Also, to begin with, be conservative as to how much filling you use, as your rice paper sheet may break if you try to overfill it; at the same time, you want to use enough filling ingredients to make a generously sized roll. Initially, it's a trial and error exercise to get the right quantity, but you'll quickly get the hang of it.

Now fold in the ends of the rice paper sheet, then roll the sheet up firmly to enclose the filling. Place your rice paper roll on a serving board or platter.

Repeat with the remaining ingredients, to make 10 rolls.

Place all the dipping sauce ingredients in a high-speed blender. Add 80 ml (2½ fl oz/⅓ cup) water and whiz until smooth. Transfer to a small serving bowl.

Serve the rice paper rolls immediately, with the dipping sauce.

250 g (9 oz) medium-firm tofu

1 beetroot (beet), peeled

2 carrots, peeled

1 Lebanese (short) cucumber

1 red capsicum (pepper)

1 yellow capsicum (pepper)

1 green capsicum (pepper)

75 g (2½ oz/1 cup) shredded purple cabbage

20 basil leaves

a handful of micro herbs

1 avocado

10 round rice paper sheets

Magic dipping sauce

4 garlic cloves, crushed

1 cm (½ inch) knob of fresh ginger, peeled and roughly chopped

45 ml (1½ fl oz) gluten-free tamari

2 tablespoons peanut or almond butter

1–2 tablespoons maple syrup

juice of 1½ limes

1 long red chilli, roughly chopped

I'm a salad-a-day kinda girl, so I don't think you can ever have too many salads in your recipe collection. This one is literally a bowl full of cancer-fighting antioxidants, fibre, vitamins, minerals and healthy fats. And go heavy-handed with the green goddess dressing — it's deliciously good for you!

I'm all for elaborate salads, but sometimes you need a quick reliable option. This raw combo is just that. Easy to prepare, full of raw goodness and addictively tasty.

Hard to believe something that tastes so good could be so great for you? Believe it.

Power salad with green goddess dressing

SERVES 2 ❌ VGN + DF + GF + RSF

1 head of broccoli, cut into florets

90 g (3¼ oz/2 cups) baby English spinach leaves

¼ small red cabbage, shredded

½ red onion, finely diced

½ avocado, peeled and cut into wedges

165 g (5¾ oz/1 cup) cooked or tinned chickpeas, rinsed and drained

2 tablespoons gluten-free tamari almonds

1 tablespoon black or white sesame seeds

Green goddess dressing

1 small avocado, peeled and stoned

1–2 garlic cloves, peeled

1 tablespoon tahini

1 tablespoon olive oil

½ cup basil leaves

½ cup flat-leaf (Italian) parsley leaves

½ teaspoon Himalayan salt

45 ml (1½ fl oz) lemon juice

45 ml (1½ fl oz) apple cider

Fill a saucepan with water and bring to the boil. Add the broccoli and blanch for 30–45 seconds, or until bright green. Remove the broccoli from the boiling water and place in a bowl of iced water to stop it cooking further. Drain and leave to dry.

Place the broccoli in a bowl with the spinach leaves, cabbage, onion, avocado and chickpeas.

Place the dressing ingredients in a high-speed blender, add 2 tablespoons water and whiz on high until smooth.

Pour your desired amount of dressing over the salad, top with the almonds and sesame seeds and serve.

Any leftover dressing will keep in the fridge for 2 days.

Beetroot, apple & fennel salad with maple walnuts

SERVES 2 ❌ VGN + DF + GF + RSF

60 g (2¼ oz/½ cup) walnuts

2 tablespoons maple syrup

1 beetroot (beet), peeled

1 fuji or gala apple

1 fennel bulb

dill sprigs or fennel fronds, to garnish

Tangy balsamic dressing

1 tablespoon olive oil

1 tablespoon balsamic vinegar

1 tablespoon dijon mustard

1–2 teaspoons maple syrup

½ teaspoon Himalayan salt, or to taste

Preheat the oven to 170°C (325°F).

Place the walnuts on a baking tray and drizzle with the maple syrup. Bake for 10 minutes, or until crispy. Remove from the oven and allow to cool.

Using a mandolin or very sharp knife, thinly slice the beetroot, apple and fennel, then arrange on a serving plate.

Combine the balsamic dressing ingredients in a bowl and mix together well. Pour the dressing over the beetroot, apple and fennel.

Top with the maple walnuts, garnish with dill or fennel fronds and dive straight in.

If you ask me what my regular meal looks like, this would be it. With its combination of all my favourite greens, this salad bowl has me hooked. My husband wonders when I'll tire of it, but I'm truly the loyal and committed type when it comes to my favourites.

Almost too yummy to be healthy, and the ultimate brunch, here is the perfect green bowl, fit for a goddess.

The green goddess bowl

SERVES 2 ⊗ VGN + DF + GF + RSF

Fill a saucepan with water and bring to the boil. Have a bowl of iced water at the ready.

Add the kale to the boiling water and blanch for 30 seconds, then remove with tongs and refresh in the iced water, to stop it cooking further.

Add the broccolini to the boiling water. Leave to boil for 1 minute, or until just tender, then remove and add to the iced water.

Blanch the beans in the boiling water for 30 seconds, then remove and add to the iced water.

Drain the blanched vegetables, then chop the kale and beans and set aside.

Warm most of the olive oil in a large frying pan over medium heat. Add the pesto, spreading it over the pan. Stir in the kale. Add the remaining olive oil, then add the broccolini and beans, stirring briefly. Stir the quinoa and lemon juice through, then remove from the heat.

Divide the rocket and zucchini among two serving bowls. Drizzle with a little extra olive oil, then top with the pesto-tossed greens.

Top with the avocado, sunflower seeds, pepitas, spring onion and basil. Sprinkle with the salt and pepper, add a lemon wedge to each bowl and enjoy.

15 g (½ oz/½ cup) shredded kale
6 broccolini stems
10 green beans
2 tablespoons olive oil, plus extra to serve
1 heaped tablespoon Pesto (page 96)
300 g (10½ oz/1½ cups) cooked quinoa
juice of ½ lemon
45 g (1½ oz/1 cup) baby rocket (arugula) leaves
1 zucchini (courgette), shredded or spiralised
1 avocado, sliced
1 tablespoon sunflower seeds
1 tablespoon pepitas (pumpkin seeds)
1 tablespoon finely chopped spring onion (scallion)
a few basil leaves
pinch of Himalayan salt
pinch of freshly ground black pepper
2 lemon wedges

All your favourite fresh flavours in one delicious salad. This salad spells summer to me: warm weather, cruisy tunes, good friends and a big platter of this poolside.

You can whip this beauty up in no time. It's fresh, light and beautifully balanced, with a tangy vinaigrette and the crunch of crisp lettuce adding the perfect finish.

Summery avo & mango salad in iceberg cups

SERVES 4 ✪ VGN + DF + GF + RSF + NF

Place the quinoa in a small saucepan with 310 ml (10¾ fl oz/1¼ cups) water and bring to the boil. Reduce the heat, then cover and simmer for 10 minutes, or until the quinoa is cooked. Set aside to cool.

Heat a gas grill or chargrill pan to high. Rub the corn with the olive oil, then grill, turning frequently, until the corn is charred and heated through. Remove from the heat and set aside to cool. When cool enough to handle, cut the kernels from the cobs.

Place the corn kernels in a large serving bowl. Add the quinoa, avocado, mango, tomatoes, mint and basil.

In a small bowl, whisk the vinaigrette ingredients together until well combined, then toss through the quinoa mixture.

Place the iceberg lettuce cups on a serving platter. Scoop the quinoa mixture into the lettuce cups, top with the spring onion and sunflower seeds and serve.

150 g (5½ oz/¾ cup) quinoa
2 corn cobs
1 teaspoon olive oil
1 avocado, sliced
1 mango, sliced
150 g (5½ oz) cherry tomatoes
1 tablespoon chopped mint
1 tablespoon chopped basil
4 iceberg lettuce leaves
1 spring onion (scallion), diced
40 g (1½ oz/¼ cup) sunflower seeds

Vinaigrette
60 ml (2 fl oz/¼ cup) extra virgin olive oil
2 tablespoons red wine vinegar
juice of 1 lime
½ teaspoon Himalayan salt, or to taste
¼ teaspoon freshly cracked black pepper

Buddha
bliss bowl 92

If I could have this Buddha bowl every day, I'd be one happy lady. A Buddha bowl is a colourful dish of raw and cooked vegies, including greens, beans, grains, seeds and a pickled or fermented item, with an insanely delicious creamy dressing. And that's exactly what this is, except I've used a lighter turmeric-spiced cauliflower 'rice' as a grain replacement, and added seared tofu steaks for extra protein.

The pickled red cabbage is so very easy, and goes with just about anything. For maximum taste, make it a day ahead. It adds a tangy zing, and brings all the yumminess together for a bowl of pure food bliss.

Buddha bliss bowl

SERVES 4 ✖ VGN + DF + GF + RSF

Easy-peasy pickled cabbage
½ red cabbage, finely shredded
250 ml (9 fl oz/1 cup) water
125 ml (4 fl oz/½ cup) apple
  cider vinegar
125 ml (4 fl oz/½ cup) red wine vinegar
2 tablespoons granulated coconut
  sugar
1 tablespoon fennel seeds
1 cm (½ inch) knob of fresh ginger,
  thinly sliced
2 garlic cloves, lightly crushed
1 teaspoon Himalayan salt
2–3 black peppercorns
2 bay leaves

Seared tofu steaks
250 g (9 oz) tofu, cut into steaks
  1 cm (½ inch) thick
1 tablespoon gluten-free tamari
1 tablespoon coconut oil

Cauliflower rice
375 g (13 oz/3 cups) cauliflower florets
1–2 teaspoons coconut oil
½ long red chilli (optional)
1 onion, finely diced
1 teaspoon finely chopped fresh ginger
1 garlic clove, crushed
1 teaspoon finely chopped fresh
  turmeric or ground turmeric
¼ teaspoon Himalayan salt
⅛ teaspoon freshly cracked black
  pepper
1 tablespoon lemon juice
1 spring onion (scallion), chopped

Sautéed spinach
2 bunches English spinach, about 200 g
  (7 oz) each, rinsed thoroughly, then
  sliced 2.5–5 cm (1–2 inches) thick
1–2 tablespoons grapeseed oil
  or olive oil
1 onion, finely diced
2 garlic cloves, crushed
¼ teaspoon Himalayan salt
⅛ teaspoon freshly cracked
  black pepper
1 tablespoon lemon juice

Buddha bliss dressing
60 ml (2 fl oz/¼ cup) olive oil
½ long red chilli
1½ tablespoons tahini
juice of 1 lemon
small handful of flat-leaf (Italian)
  parsley leaves
½ teaspoon Himalayan salt

Assembling the bowl
6–8 broccolini stems, trimmed
  and lightly steamed
165 g (5¾ oz/1 cup) cooked or
  tinned chickpeas
1 avocado, sliced
1 tablespoon pepitas (pumpkin seeds),
  lightly toasted
1 tablespoon lightly toasted pine nuts
  (optional; omit for a nut-free dish)

Easy-peasy pickled cabbage

Combine all the ingredients in a clean 2 litre (70 fl oz/8 cup) jar. Leave at room temperature on your kitchen bench for 2–3 hours, then transfer to the fridge overnight.

You will notice that the liquid does not cover the cabbage at first, but as it sits, the cabbage will shrink and the liquid will eventually cover it.

The pickled cabbage will keep in the fridge for up to 4 weeks.

Seared tofu steaks

Put the tofu steaks in a wide shallow bowl. Drizzle with half the tamari, then turn the tofu over and drizzle the other side.

Melt the coconut oil in a large frying pan over medium heat.

Add the tofu and sizzle on each side for 1–2 minutes, or until lightly browned. Set aside.

Cauliflower rice

In a food processor, and working in batches, process the cauliflower florets in short bursts until the cauliflower resembles rice grains. You don't want the cauliflower to be super fine or chunky, so use the pulse function to control the process. Set aside.

Melt the coconut oil in a large frying pan over medium heat. Add the chilli and onion and sauté for 2–3 minutes. Add the ginger and garlic and sauté until fragrant, then add the cauliflower. Stir well, adding the turmeric, salt and pepper.

Remove from the heat, add the lemon juice and spring onion and toss together. Set aside.

Sautéed spinach

Bring a large saucepan of water to the boil. Add the spinach and allow to boil for 2–3 minutes, or until the leaves are just tender.

Drain the spinach well, then firmly squeeze all the water from the spinach. You can use your hands, or wring the spinach in a tea towel to squeeze out all the water.

Heat the oil in a frying pan over medium heat. Add the onion and sauté for 2–3 minutes, or until translucent and fragrant. Add the garlic and stir until fragrant.

Fold the chopped spinach through, then stir in the salt, pepper and lemon juice. Remove from the heat and set aside.

Buddha bliss dressing

Place all the dressing ingredients in a high-speed blender.

Add 125 ml (4 fl oz/½ cup) water and whiz until smooth. If the dressing is too thick to process easily, blend in a little more water.

To assemble the Buddha bowl

Arrange the broccolini, chickpeas, avocado, sautéed spinach, cauliflower rice, seared tofu and pickled cabbage in serving bowls.

Top with the toasted pepitas and pine nuts, drizzle with the Buddha bliss dressing and serve.

I bet you have some preconceptions about vegie burgers. I think we can safely say we've all had our fair share of bad experiences.

What if I can turn things around and assure you that this recipe will make you forget about all those dry, flaky patties you've tasted in the past? I'd even suggest you could convince your sceptic friends into trying one, too! Full of flavour and nutrition, these vegie delights will satisfy your deepest burger cravings.

This easy recipe is a definite keeper. Try it and see.

Vegie burgers

SERVES 5 ✪ VGN + DF + GF + RSF + NF

Preheat the oven to 180°C (350°F). Line a baking tray with baking paper.

To make the patties, place the sweet potato in a food processor with the corn and chickpeas. Pulse until the mixture is smooth, but with some chunky bits for texture.

Heat 1 tablespoon of the olive oil in a saucepan and sauté the onion and garlic for 2–3 minutes. Remove from the heat and allow to cool slightly, then add the onion mixture to the processor and pulse until combined.

Transfer the mixture to a bowl. Add the quinoa flakes, parsley, cumin, paprika, turmeric, salt and pepper and mix until well combined.

In a small bowl, whisk the linseed meal with 60 ml (2 fl oz/¼ cup) water. Using your hands (food-handling gloves are useful here!), incorporate the linseed mixture into the spiced vegie mixture.

Shape the mixture into five patties, about 2.5 cm (1 inch) thick and 13 cm (5 inches) in diameter, and place on a sheet of baking paper.

Heat the remaining tablespoon of olive oil in a large frying pan. Working in batches, cook the patties on each side for 2–3 minutes, or until nicely browned.

Transfer the patties to the baking tray, then into the oven. Bake for 25–30 minutes, or until cooked through.

Just before serving, place all the avocado mayo ingredients in a blender and whiz until smooth.

Cut the burger buns open and place some shredded lettuce on the bottom half of each bun.

Add the burger patties, some avocado mayo, tomato, onion and cucumber. Add some jalapeño chilli and a dollop of mustard, if using. Dollop with more mayo and devour!

Patties

1 orange sweet potato, peeled and cut into chunks, then steamed or roasted until tender

200 g (7 oz/1 cup) fresh (or well-drained tinned) corn kernels, or 150 g (5½ oz/ 1 cup) frozen corn kernels, thawed

250 g (9 oz/1½ cups) cooked or tinned chickpeas, rinsed and drained

2 tablespoons olive oil

1 brown onion, finely diced

1 garlic clove, crushed

3 tablespoons quinoa flakes

3 tablespoons chopped flat-leaf (Italian) parsley

½ teaspoon ground cumin

½ teaspoon hot paprika

¼ teaspoon ground turmeric

1 teaspoon Himalayan salt, or to taste

½ teaspoon freshly cracked black pepper

2 tablespoons linseed (flaxseed) meal

To assemble

5 gluten-free seeded buns

½ iceberg lettuce, shredded

1 tomato, sliced

1 red onion, cut into thin rounds

1 Lebanese (short) cucumber, sliced

1 tablespoon jalapeño chillies (optional)

1 tablespoon American mustard (optional)

Avocado mayo

flesh of 1 large avocado

2 tablespoons extra virgin olive oil

1 garlic clove, crushed

juice of ½ lemon

½ teaspoon dijon mustard

¼ teaspoon Himalayan salt

¼ teaspoon hot paprika

I'll often grill up a mix of classic Mediterranean vegetables to enjoy throughout the week, as they go beautifully in so many different meals — including this salad, which is one of my favourites. It also includes some roasted sweet potato and the ever-versatile quinoa, as well as a spin on my pesto and a no-cheese sauce to make this dish a true flavour knockout.

Chargrilled vegetable salad with quinoa, pesto & cheesy sauce

SERVES 2 ⊗ VGN + DF + GF + RSF

Preheat the oven to 170°C (325°F).

Coat the sweet potato with 1–2 teaspoons of the coconut oil and spread on a baking tray. Transfer to the oven and bake for 20–25 minutes, or until cooked through. Remove from the oven and set aside.

Meanwhile, heat a barbecue or chargrill pan to medium–high. In a small bowl, combine the garlic, salt and remaining coconut oil. Brush the mixture over the eggplant, capsicum and zucchini slices.

Working in batches if necessary, grill the eggplant, capsicum and zucchini slices for 2–3 minutes on each side, or until cooked through. Remove from the heat.

Add the sweet potato slices to the grill and brown each side briefly. Remove from the heat.

In a mixing bowl, combine the spinach leaves, parsley and cooked quinoa. Combine the olive oil, lemon juice and salt, drizzle over the salad and toss.

Arrange the salad and chargrilled vegetables on a platter. Top with the pine nuts. Serve with the pesto and cheesy sauce.

Pesto

Place the pine nuts in a food processor and pulse until large crumbs form.

Add the garlic, basil, rocket, salt, pepper and lemon juice. Pulse until just combined. Add the olive oil and process until smooth.

The pesto is best made just before serving, but will keep in the fridge for a day or two in an airtight container, covered with a layer of olive oil to stop the basil discolouring.

Cheesy sauce

Drain the cashews and place in a high-speed food processor with the lemon juice. Blend until the nuts have broken down into fine pieces.

Add the remaining ingredients, pour in 125 ml (4 fl oz/½ cup) water and process until smooth, adding a little more water if required.

This sauce is best made near serving time.

TIP *It's important to use a mild-tasting olive oil (often labelled 'light' olive oil) in the pesto, to avoid a heavy, unpalatable result.*

1 medium sweet potato, cut into 1 cm (½ inch) rounds
1½ tablespoons melted coconut oil, for brushing
1 garlic clove, crushed
⅛ teaspoon Himalayan salt
1 eggplant (aubergine), cut into 1 cm (½ inch) rounds
1 capsicum (pepper), cut into long thick slices, along its natural ridges
2 zucchini (courgettes), sliced 5 mm (¼ inch) thick
45 g (1½ oz/1 cup) baby English spinach leaves
3 tablespoons finely chopped flat-leaf (Italian) parsley
100 g (3½ oz/½ cup) quinoa, cooked
1 tablespoon extra virgin olive oil
2 tablespoons lemon juice
¼ teaspoon Himalayan salt, or to taste
2 tablespoons toasted pine nuts

Pesto
115 g (4 oz/¾ cup) pine nuts
2 garlic cloves, peeled
¾ cup basil leaves, loosely packed
25 g (1 oz/1 cup) rocket (arugula) leaves
½ teaspoon Himalayan salt, or to taste
¼ teaspoon freshly ground black pepper
juice of 1 lemon
250 ml (9 fl oz/1 cup) mild-tasting olive oil (see tip)

Cheesy sauce
150 g (5½ oz/1 cup) cashews, soaked overnight
60 ml (2 fl oz/¼ cup) lemon juice
25 g (1 oz/½ cup) nutritional yeast
2 garlic cloves, peeled
½ teaspoon onion powder
1 tablespoon dijon mustard
½ teaspoon Himalayan salt, or to taste

If you don't like kale or don't know how to incorporate it into your diet, this salad will help you on your way.

This is the salad you have when you don't really feel like a salad. The one that tastes way more exciting than it should, and the one you'll keep going back to for that very reason. And you don't need a whole heap of ingredients for it — just some time to get yourself sorted.

Once it all comes together, you'll be in love.

Kale, quinoa & sweet potato salad

SERVES 2 ✪ VGN + DF + GF + RSF

Preheat the oven to 170°C (325°F). Coat the sweet potato with the coconut oil, place on a baking tray and bake for 20–25 minutes, or until cooked through.

Meanwhile, place the quinoa in a small saucepan with 310 ml (10¾ fl oz/1¼ cups) water and bring to the boil. Reduce the heat, then cover and simmer for 10 minutes, or until the quinoa is cooked.

Place the roasted sweet potato in a large bowl, along with the quinoa, kale, mint, parsley and onion. Gently mix together.

To make the dressing, whisk the tahini and lemon juice in a small bowl until combined. Whisk in the pomegranate molasses, salt and 1–2 tablespoons water until smooth. Taste and add the maple syrup if you'd like it a little sweeter.

Pour the dressing over the salad, top with the almonds and pepitas and serve.

TIP When baking the sweet potato, you could roast up an extra quantity at the same time, to use in other dishes such as the Chargrilled vegetable salad (page 96), Tofu balls (page 130) and Vegie burgers (page 94).

150 g (5½ oz/1 cup) chopped orange sweet potato (see tip)
1–2 teaspoons melted coconut oil
150 g (5½ oz/¾ cup) quinoa
100 g (2½ oz/1½ cups, firmly packed) shredded kale
3 tablespoons finely chopped mint leaves
3 tablespoons finely chopped flat-leaf (Italian) parsley
½ red onion, diced
40 g (1½ oz/¼ cup) gluten-free tamari almonds, chopped
2 tablespoons pepitas (pumpkin seeds)

Dressing
1 tablespoon tahini
2 tablespoons lemon juice
1 tablespoon pomegranate molasses
½ teaspoon Himalayan salt, or to taste
1 teaspoon maple syrup (optional)

Clockwise, from right:
Crackers *102*

×

White bean &
artichoke dip *102*

×

Beetroot hummus *102*

Rocket pesto *102*

SNACK PLATTER

**Crackers and dips to
step up your snack game**

Originally I planned this recipe around my favourite snack option: these super-addictive crackers with a few beautiful fresh toppings. But as I started experimenting with different toppings and dips with the crackers, they all tasted so good I decided to offer you a full snack platter instead! Enjoy.

Snack platter

SERVES 4 ⊗ VGN + DF + GF + RSF

Crackers

150 g (5½ oz/1 cup) linseeds (flaxseeds)
40 g (1½ oz/¼ cup) chia seeds
40 g (1½ oz/¼ cup) sesame seeds
30 g (1 oz/¼ cup) sunflower seeds
½ teaspoon onion powder
½ teaspoon garlic powder
½ teaspoon Himalayan salt, or to taste
¼ teaspoon dried parsley flakes
¼ teaspoon hot paprika or chilli powder
 (optional)

Beetroot hummus

1 small beetroot (beet), scrubbed clean
45 ml (1½ fl oz) olive oil, plus extra for
 drizzling
250 g (9 oz/1½ cups) cooked chickpeas,
 or 400 g (14 oz) tinned chickpeas,
 rinsed and drained
juice of 1 lemon
2 tablespoons tahini
2 garlic cloves, peeled
½ teaspoon ground cumin
¼ teaspoon Himalayan salt, or to taste

Rocket pesto

75 g (2½ oz/½ cup) pine nuts
90 g (3¼ oz/2 cups) rocket (arugula)
 leaves
15 g (½ oz/¼ cup, firmly packed) basil
 leaves
1 garlic clove, peeled
60 ml (2 fl oz/¼ cup) mild-tasting
 olive oil
juice of 1 lemon
½ teaspoon Himalayan salt, or to taste

White bean & artichoke dip

400 g (14 oz/1½ cups) cooked cannellini
 beans, or a 440 g (15½ oz) tin
 cannellini beans, rinsed and drained
400 g (14 oz) tin artichoke hearts, rinsed
 and drained
1 teaspoon finely grated lemon zest
juice of 1 lemon
2 garlic cloves, peeled
¼ teaspoon chilli powder
¼ teaspoon ground cumin
½ teaspoon Himalayan salt, or to taste
⅛ teaspoon freshly ground black pepper

To serve

4–6 vine-ripened tomatoes, chopped
1 avocado, sliced

For the crackers

Preheat the oven to 150°C (300°F). Line a baking tray with baking paper.

Combine the linseeds and chia seeds in a bowl. Add 250 ml (9 fl oz/ 1 cup) water and allow to sit for 20–30 minutes.

In a separate bowl, place the sesame seeds, sunflower seeds, onion powder, garlic powder, salt and parsley. Add the paprika or chilli powder, if using.

Things will get a bit sticky here, so I suggest slipping on a pair of food-handling gloves at this point. Using your hands, mix the soaked seeds into the dry ingredients, then spread the mixture over the prepared baking tray, flattening it out; the mixture will be slimy and sticky. I like my crackers fairly thin — about 2–3 mm ($1/16$–$1/8$ inch) — but their thickness is a personal choice. Now lightly score the mixture into squares or wedges with a knife.

Bake for 55–65 minutes, then flip the mixture over and bake for a further 55–65 minutes, or until firm and crispy.

Allow to cool, before snapping into squares or wedges. The crackers will keep in an airtight container in the pantry for 2–4 weeks.

For the beetroot hummus

Preheat the oven to 180°C (350°F). Place the beetroot on a piece of baking paper, then a piece of foil. Drizzle with a little olive oil, sprinkle with a pinch of salt and wrap up tightly. Place on a baking tray and bake for 45–60 minutes, or until tender.

Remove from the oven and leave until cool enough to handle, then peel off the skin. Place the beetroot in a food processor, along with the 45 ml (1½ fl oz) olive oil. Add the remaining hummus ingredients and process until smooth, then transfer to a bowl.

The hummus will keep in the fridge in an airtight container for 4–5 days.

For the rocket pesto

Place the pine nuts in a small dry frying pan over medium heat, shaking the pan for a minute or two so they toast evenly. As soon as they have browned, tip them into a food processor and blend for a few seconds, until the nuts have broken down into small crumbs.

Add the rocket and basil and garlic and process briefly. Add the olive oil, lemon juice and salt and blend until smooth.

Covered with a layer of olive oil, the pesto will keep in the fridge in an airtight container for 2–3 days.

For the bean & artichoke dip

Place the beans and artichoke hearts in a food processor and process until well combined.

Add the lemon zest, lemon juice and garlic and process until smooth. You may need to add 2 tablespoons water if your mixture is dry.

Add the remaining ingredients and process briefly.

The dip will keep in the fridge in an airtight container for 2–3 days.

To assemble the platter

Just before serving, arrange the crackers, dips, tomatoes and avocado on a large platter. Graze to your heart's content.

When I first experimented with scrambled tofu, this spicy combination really took me by surprise. Tofu is filling and satisfying, and with a selection of vegie sides becomes a standout meal that will keep you going all day.

Turmeric is the hero here and is the secret to the tofu's yellow colour. It is considered a potential cancer-fighting spice and is used as an anti-inflammatory in Chinese and Indian medicine. Curcumin, the main active compound in turmeric, is also showing promise as an anti-depressant — as though you needed any further incentive to get into the kitchen and get cooking!

Scrambled tofu

SERVES 2 ✪ VGN + DF + GF + RSF + NF

Preheat the oven to 180°C (350°F). Line a baking tray with baking paper. Cut the tomatoes in half and place on the baking tray, cut side up. Add the mushrooms, gill side up.

In a small bowl, combine the garlic, olive oil and salt. Drizzle over the tomatoes and mushrooms and bake for 15–20 minutes, or until cooked. Remove from the oven and keep warm.

Meanwhile, heat the grapeseed oil in a large saucepan. Add the kale and sauté over medium heat for a few minutes, until wilted but not soggy. Stir in the lemon juice, remove the kale from the pan and keep warm.

To prepare the tofu, heat the grapeseed oil in the saucepan, add the onion and sauté over medium heat for a few minutes. Add the garlic and chilli and cook briefly, then add the turmeric and sauté until fragrant. Stir the tofu through.

Add the cumin, paprika, salt and pepper and stir well until the mixture resembles a scramble. Stir in the coconut milk and remove from the heat.

Serve immediately, with the warm kale, mushrooms and tomatoes.

3 tomatoes
2 field mushrooms
1 garlic clove, crushed
1 tablespoon olive oil
⅛ teaspoon Himalayan salt
1 tablespoon grapeseed oil
100 g (3½ oz/2 cups) baby kale leaves
1 tablespoon lemon juice

Spiced tofu
1 tablespoon grapeseed oil
1 small brown onion, diced
2 garlic cloves, crushed
1 red chilli, chopped (optional)
1 cm (½ inch) knob of fresh turmeric, peeled and grated, or 2 teaspoons ground turmeric
300 g (10½ oz) medium-firm tofu, drained and chopped into 1 cm (½ inch) cubes
1 teaspoon ground cumin
¼ teaspoon hot paprika
¼ teaspoon Himalayan salt, or to taste
¼ teaspoon freshly cracked black pepper
2–3 tablespoons coconut milk

*Pumpkin, quinoa, spinach, mushrooms and chickpeas,
all in the one dish — the best baked pumpkin ever.
I often share this meal with my mum, as she, too, loves
to combine all her favourite ingredients in the one meal.
She calls it party food — maybe because it's 'party in your
mouth' kind of stuff. Whatever the reason, I'm into it.
Hope you are too.*

The best baked pumpkin ever

SERVES 4 ✪ VGN + DF + GF + RSF

Preheat the oven to 180°C (350°F). Cut the pumpkin into quarters and remove the seeds. Place on a baking tray or in a baking dish.

Combine 1 tablespoon of the oil with the thyme leaves and salt, then massage over the pumpkin quarters. Transfer to the oven and bake for about 50 minutes, or until the pumpkin is lightly browned and tender when tested with a sharp knife.

Meanwhile, heat the remaining 1 tablespoon oil in a large frying pan over medium heat. Sauté the leek for 2–3 minutes, or until translucent. Add the chilli and garlic and sauté for a further 1–2 minutes.

Stir the mushrooms through and sauté briefly, then add the spinach leaves and cook until the spinach has wilted and all the vegetables are nicely coated. Stir in the stock, quinoa and chickpeas and allow to heat through for about 2–3 minutes. Add the salt, pepper and lemon juice and remove from the heat.

In a small frying pan, toast the almonds over medium heat for 2–3 minutes, or until lightly browned. Set aside.

When the pumpkin is ready, remove from the oven and arrange on a serving board. Scoop the quinoa mixture into each pumpkin quarter. Add a drizzle of olive oil and garnish with the toasted almonds.

Serve immediately, with lemon wedges for squeezing over.

TIP *For a nut-free meal, you could use pepitas (pumpkin seeds) instead of the almonds.*

1 medium-sized jap or kent pumpkin

2 tablespoons olive oil or grapeseed oil

1 teaspoon thyme leaves

¼ teaspoon Himalayan salt

1 tablespoon chopped leek, white part only

½ long red chilli (optional)

2 garlic cloves, crushed

100 g (3½ oz) whole or halved Swiss brown mushrooms

45 g (1½ oz/1 cup) baby English spinach leaves

1–2 tablespoons vegetable stock

200 g (7 oz/1 cup) cooked quinoa

85 g (3 oz/½ cup) cooked or tinned chickpeas

½ teaspoon Himalayan salt, or to taste

¼ teaspoon freshly ground black pepper

1 tablespoon lemon juice

2 tablespoons slivered almonds (see tip)

1 tablespoon extra virgin olive oil

lemon wedges, to serve

We fight over sushi at our house. We all love it... but who doesn't? Sushi is just the perfect lunch or snack.

Instead of using traditional sticky white sushi rice, I use quinoa and the tiniest bit of coconut sugar, which tastes just as good, and is much healthier. I also love its nutty flavour, and the simple sweet-salty combination of avocado, cucumber, corn and tamari.

We love it as is, but you can be creative and add other vegies and wasabi if you please.

Quinoa sushi

SERVES 2–4 ✖ VGN + DF + GF + RSF + NF

Combine the quinoa and salt in a saucepan. Add 750 ml (26 fl oz/ 3 cups) water and bring to the boil. Cover the pan, reduce the heat to low and simmer for 15–20 minutes, or until the quinoa is tender and the water is absorbed.

Transfer the quinoa to a bowl, add the combined vinegar and coconut sugar, then set aside to cool.

Lay a bamboo sushi mat over a clean chopping board. (To stop the nori sticking to the bamboo, you can also spread a sheet of plastic wrap over the sushi mat at this point.)

Place a nori sheet, shiny side down, on the sushi mat. Evenly spread one-quarter of the quinoa mixture in a thin layer all over the nori sheet, leaving about 2 cm (¾ inch) of nori clear on the top edge, and lightly pressing the quinoa onto the nori.

Arrange one-quarter of the cucumber, avocado and corn over the quinoa, in a line down the centre.

Lift one end of the sushi mat and start to roll the nori firmly over the filling, pressing down. Lift the mat a little and press into the roll, to ensure it has held well, then reposition the mat and roll again firmly towards the other end of the nori, creating one long roll. Moisten the end of the nori with water to help it adhere to the roll, and hold it all together. Set aside.

Continue with the remaining nori sheets, vegetables and quinoa, to make another three rolls.

Using a sharp wet knife, cut each nori roll into 6–8 pieces. Arrange on a platter or individual serving plates, cut side up, with a small side dish of tamari, and pickled ginger if desired.

Enjoy straightaway.

300 g (10½ oz/1½ cups) quinoa
⅛ teaspoon Himalayan salt
45 ml (1½ fl oz) rice vinegar
¼ teaspoon granulated coconut sugar
4 nori sheets
2 Lebanese (short) cucumbers, seeds removed, then cut into thin matchsticks
1 avocado, sliced
2 cooked corn cobs, kernels removed
45 ml (1½ fl oz) gluten-free tamari
2 tablespoons pickled ginger (optional)

I adore the appearance of luscious, juicy figs at my local farmers' market each autumn. It means I have just a few months to make this fresh fig salad on repeat.

This is such a simple recipe, in which the partnership of plump figs, creamy avocado and juicy tomatoes is king. Drizzle with a fresh basil dressing and the flavours really sing. Cherish each and every mouthful.

Sexy fig salad with basil dressing

SERVES 2 ✕ VGN + DF + GF + RSF + NF

Arrange the salad leaves and sliced figs, tomatoes and avocado on two serving plates.

Combine the basil dressing ingredients in a blender and whiz until smooth.

Drizzle the salads with the dressing, then garnish with basil leaves and serve.

TIP If you like pine nuts, you could sprinkle a small handful of lightly toasted pine nuts over the salad just before serving, although of course the recipe will no longer be nut free.

50 g (1¾ oz/1 cup) mixed salad leaves
5–6 figs, sliced
4 tomatoes, sliced
1 avocado, sliced
basil leaves, to garnish

Basil dressing
60 ml (2 fl oz/¼ cup) extra virgin olive oil
2 tablespoons balsamic vinegar
15 basil leaves
1 garlic clove, peeled
½ teaspoon Himalayan salt, or to taste
¼ teaspoon freshly ground black
    pepper

SOUP'S ON!

**Nourishing soups
that turn up the heat**

Clockwise from top:
Spiced carrot
& lentil soup *115*

×

Roasted cinnamon
pumpkin soup *119*

×

Minty pea soup with spiced
crunchy edamame beans *118*

×

Lentil & silverbeet soup *114*

This warming soup was a favourite of my parents, heavily influenced by flavours from their culture. It didn't really appeal to me when I was younger — not for a long time.

As an adult, I now appreciate it wholeheartedly. The simple coming together of all the flavours, and its smooth yet chunky texture, make it a deeply soul-nourishing soup.

Lentil & silverbeet soup

SERVES 4 ⊗ VGN + DF + GF + RSF + NF

Rinse the lentils and place in a saucepan. Pour in 750 ml (26 fl oz/ 3 cups) water and bring to the boil.

Stir in the cumin, salt and pepper. Add the silverbeet, reduce the heat and simmer, uncovered, for 20–30 minutes, or until the silverbeet is tender; about halfway through cooking, stir in an extra 125–250 ml (4–9 fl oz/½–1 cup) water, depending on how thick you like your soup.

Remove from the heat. Using a hand-held stick blender, blend the soup until half of it is smooth, but chunkier bits remain. Keep warm.

In a frying pan, heat the oil over medium heat, then sauté the onion for 2–3 minutes, or until translucent. Add the garlic and sauté for a further 1–2 minutes.

Stir the lemon juice into the soup, then ladle into serving bowls. Top with the sautéed onion mixture, sprinkle with the chilli powder and serve.

TIP *Traditionally this is enjoyed with lots of lemon juice stirred in before serving. Add less or more lemon juice to suit your own taste.*

200 g (7 oz/1 cup) dried red lentils
½ teaspoon ground cumin
½ teaspoon Himalayan salt, or to taste
¼ teaspoon freshly ground black pepper
2 handfuls chopped silverbeet (Swiss chard) leaves, stalks removed
1 tablespoon coconut oil or grapeseed oil
1 onion, finely diced
1 garlic clove, crushed
juice of 1–2 lemons (see tip)
½ teaspoon chilli powder

I've been making this spiced carrot and lentil soup for my family since forever. It's an easy throw-together that hits the spot each time, and best of all provides all the nourishment and cosy comfort vibes that you expect from a soup.

Spiced carrot & lentil soup

SERVES 4 ✕ VGN + DF + GF + RSF + NF

Melt the coconut oil in a large saucepan and sauté the onion and chilli over medium heat for 2–3 minutes, or until the onion is translucent.

Stir in the garlic and ginger and sauté for a further 1–2 minutes, or until fragrant. Add the carrots and stir briefly. Sprinkle with the turmeric, cumin, salt and pepper, then stir in the tomatoes, vegetable stock and lentils.

Bring to the boil, then reduce the heat, cover and simmer for 30–35 minutes, or until the lentils are tender.

Ladle the soup into serving bowls. Top with the coconut yoghurt and crispy chickpeas and serve.

1–2 tablespoons coconut oil
1 onion, finely diced
1 long red chilli, finely chopped
2 garlic cloves
1 teaspoon finely chopped or grated fresh ginger
2 carrots, peeled and chopped
½ teaspoon ground turmeric
⅓ teaspoon ground cumin
½ teaspoon Himalayan salt, or to taste
¼ teaspoon freshly ground black pepper
400 g (14 oz) tin chopped tomatoes
750 ml (26 fl oz/3 cups) vegetable stock
200 g (7 oz/1 cup) dried red lentils, rinsed
140 g (5 oz/½ cup) unsweetened coconut yoghurt
Crispy spiced chickpeas (page 136), to serve

EAT WELL,
TRAVEL OFTEN

Anything peas and I'm in. Of all the soups, this is probably my favourite, as it's light, totally healthy and loved by all, and also very simple to prepare.

When I'm struggling to think what to make for dinner, I can always count on this one as I almost always have the ingredients on hand, and it's made in no time.

Just how I like it.

Minty pea soup with spiced crunchy edamame beans

SERVES 6 ⊗ VGN + DF + GF + RSF + NF

Melt the coconut oil in a large saucepan over medium heat. Add the leek and onion and sauté for 2–3 minutes, or until the onion is translucent and fragrant. Add the garlic and sauté for a further 1–2 minutes.

Stir in the stock, mint, salt and pepper and bring to the boil. Add the potato and allow to boil for 5–6 minutes, or until the potato is just tender.

Stir in the peas and bring to a light boil.

Allow the soup to cool slightly, then transfer to a high-speed blender and process until smooth. Return to the saucepan and gently reheat before serving.

For the spiced crunchy edamame
Preheat the oven to 180°C (350°F). Line a baking tray with baking paper.

Bring a large saucepan of water to the boil. Add the edamame and allow to boil for just 1 minute, then drain.

Remove the edamame beans from their shells and place in a bowl. Add the coconut oil and spices and gently toss to coat evenly.

Transfer to the baking tray and bake for 12–15 minutes, or until the edamame are roasted and browned. Remove from the oven.

To serve
Ladle the warm soup into serving bowls and add a small dollop or swirl of coconut cream, if desired. Top with the edamame beans, sprinkle with the chilli powder and serve.

2–3 tablespoons coconut oil
2 tablespoons finely chopped leek, white part only
1 onion, finely diced
2 garlic cloves, crushed
1 litre (35 fl oz/4 cups) vegetable stock
25–30 g (1 oz/½–¾ cup) chopped mint leaves
½–1 teaspoon Himalayan salt, or to taste
⅛ teaspoon freshly ground black pepper
2 potatoes, peeled and chopped
800 g (1 lb 12 oz) fresh or frozen peas
2 tablespoons coconut cream (optional)
½ teaspoon chilli powder

Spiced crunchy edamame
400 g (14 oz) frozen edamame (green soy beans)
1–2 teaspoons melted coconut oil
¼ teaspoon onion powder
¼ teaspoon garlic powder
¼ teaspoon ground cumin
¼ teaspoon hot paprika
¼ teaspoon Himalayan salt
⅛ teaspoon freshly ground black pepper

Out-of-this-world delicious, cinnamon pumpkin has to be tried to be believed. Cinnamon brings out the sweetness in the pumpkin, making this soup irresistible.

Pumpkin is such a versatile, nutritious, low-kilojoule, fibre-rich vegie that it's a staple in my diet. I like to bake my pumpkin to get maximum flavour for this wonderful soup, and it definitely pays off — yum!

Roasted cinnamon pumpkin soup

SERVES 4 ⊗ VGN + DF + GF + RSF + NF

Start by roasting the pumpkin. Preheat the oven to 180ºC (350ºF).

Combine the coconut oil, cinnamon and salt and massage the mixture over the pumpkin wedges. Spread them on a baking tray lined with baking paper and bake for 20–25 minutes, or until tender and nicely browned. Remove from the oven and leave to cool slightly, then peel off the skin.

Meanwhile, melt the coconut oil in a large saucepan over medium heat. Sauté the onion for 2–3 minutes, or until translucent, then add the garlic and sauté for a further 1–2 minutes. Stir in the stock, cloves, cinnamon stick, chilli, salt and pepper. Add the pumpkin and bring to the boil, then reduce the heat and simmer, uncovered, for 20–25 minutes.

Remove the cinnamon stick and cloves. Allow to cool slightly, then transfer the soup to a food processor. Blend until completely smooth. Gently reheat before serving.

To make the crunchy quinoa, melt the coconut oil in a frying pan over medium heat, add the quinoa and stir frequently until toasted and crispy; this may take around 5–7 minutes.

In a small frying pan, dry fry the pepitas for 2–3 minutes, until lightly toasted. Immediately remove from the heat.

Ladle the hot soup into serving bowls. Top each with the toasted pepita seeds and crunchy quinoa. Sprinkle with cinnamon if desired and serve.

1 tablespoon melted coconut oil

1 onion, finely diced

2 garlic cloves, crushed

500 ml (17 fl oz/2 cups) vegetable stock

5–6 cloves

½ cinnamon stick

½ teaspoon chilli powder (optional)

½ teaspoon Himalayan salt, or to taste

¼ teaspoon freshly ground black pepper

75 g (2½ oz/½ cup) pepitas (pumpkin seeds)

ground cinnamon, for sprinkling (optional)

Cinnamon pumpkin

1 medium jap or kent pumpkin, cut into wedges

2 tablespoons coconut oil

½ teaspoon ground cinnamon

⅛ teaspoon Himalayan salt

Crunchy quinoa

1–2 teaspoons coconut oil

200 g (7 oz/1 cup) cooked quinoa

Stuffed vine leaves are a cherished family recipe, always disappearing in seconds at our special get-togethers, met with hungry eagerness by members young and old.

Here, as always, I've altered our traditional recipe for extra health benefits, using brown rice instead of white, more herbs and spices, and a handful of walnuts for the perfect nutty texture — but you could leave the walnuts out if you'd like these dainty morsels to be nut free.

This one's special to me. Please pay close attention to all the steps to ensure you get the best results, so you love it as much as we do.

Stuffed vine leaves

MAKES 40 ✖ VGN + DF + GF + RSF

Bring the rice and 375 ml (13 fl oz/ 1½ cups) water to the boil in a saucepan. Reduce the heat, cover and simmer for about 15 minutes, or until the water is absorbed and the rice is cooked. Set aside to cool.

Heat the olive oil in a frying pan over medium heat. Add the onion and sauté for a few minutes, until the oil is bubbling and the onion is transparent. Set a fine-mesh strainer over a bowl, then tip the onion and oil mixture into the strainer. Reserve the onion-flavoured oil for drizzling over the rolled vine leaves.

Tip the sautéed onion into a bowl. Add the cooled rice and sprinkle with the pepper, 1 teaspoon of the salt, and ½ teaspoon of the cumin. Add the parsley, dill, currants, walnuts and pomegranate molasses and mix until well combined.

If using fresh leaves, blanch them in a bowl of boiling water for 1–2 minutes, allowing the leaves to soften; be careful not to soak them too long, or they will become too delicate to use. Now soak the leaves in cold water and drain, ready to use. If using preserved leaves from a jar or can, soak them in boiling water for a few minutes, then cold water for a few minutes, then repeat the soaking

process a second time, to fully rinse off all the salt and vinegar.

Take a vine leaf and briefly pat dry with paper towel. Place on a large chopping board, shiny side down. Place 1 tablespoon of the rice mixture along the base of the leaf. Fold in both sides of the leaf, then roll up tightly, away from you. Repeat with the remaining leaves and rice mixture, to make about 40 rolls.

Tightly pack the stuffed leaves into a deep, 28 cm (11¼ inch) frying pan. Combine the reserved onion-flavoured oil and lemon juice with the remaining ½ teaspoon salt and ¼ teaspoon cumin and drizzle over the stacked leaves.

Weigh the leaves down with a large heatproof plate, so they don't unravel during cooking. Place a heavy object, such as a mortar or several cans of food, on top of the plate to keep the leaves in place. Bring the pan to the boil, then reduce the heat and simmer, without the lid on, for 45–60 minutes, or until the rice is cooked when tasted.

Leave to cool, then refrigerate in an airtight container overnight. The stuffed vine leaves are best served cold from the fridge the next day. They will keep for up to 4–5 days.

220 g (8 oz/1 cup) medium-grain
  brown rice
250 ml (9 fl oz/1 cup) olive oil
3 brown onions, finely diced
¼ teaspoon freshly ground
  black pepper
1½ teaspoons Himalayan salt
¾ teaspoon ground cumin
15 g (½ oz/½ cup) finely chopped
  flat-leaf (Italian) parsley
1 tablespoon finely chopped dill
2 tablespoons currants
30 g (1 oz/¼ cup) walnuts, chopped
1–2 teaspoons pomegranate molasses
40 medium-sized grape vine leaves
  (see tip)
125 ml (4½ fl oz/½ cup) lemon juice

TIP *Fresh grape vine leaves really make this dish. In summer you may be able to source them through your local deli or Mediterranean grocer; thankfully you'll find good alternatives preserved in jars year round. Choose medium-sized vine leaves: large ones are often too tough, and small ones are fiddly to work with. As a simple guide, use leaves that are slightly smaller than an average hand. Discard any leaves with holes in them.*

Middle Eastern street food just got a health lift!
Za'atar, an ancient Middle Eastern health spice, was a staple in my home growing up. We used it in many different ways, but by far the most delicious was to bake it over home-made bread or pizza dough — an absolute taste sensation. We'd been desperately missing za'atar bread (also known as mana'eesh*) until I found the right dough replacement. This recipe uses a cauliflower base, and is a dream come true.*

Za'atar breads

MAKES ABOUT 12 ✪ VGN + DF + GF + RSF + NF

Preheat the oven to 180°C (350°F). Line a 40 x 28 cm (16 x 11 inch) baking tray with baking paper.

Cut the cauliflower into florets and remove the thick stems. Working in batches, process the cauliflower florets in a food processor until they resemble crumbs.

Bring a small saucepan of water to the boil. Add the cauliflower crumbs and cook for 2–3 minutes, or until lightly cooked. Drain into a strainer and allow to cool.

Tip the cauliflower into a clean tea towel, wrap it into a bundle and wring firmly to squeeze out as much water as possible. You will notice lots of water draining; keep going until all the water is completely gone.

Empty the cauliflower into a bowl. Add the sorghum flour, psyllium husks, onion powder, garlic powder and salt and mix until well combined.

Put the linseed meal in a bowl and stir in 170 ml (5½ fl oz/⅔ cup) water. Add to the cauliflower mixture and combine well — it's a good idea to slip on some food-handling gloves here! — until your mixture resembles a dough.

Spread the cauliflower dough over the baking tray. Firmly press the rim of an upturned 8 cm (3¼ inch) bowl or cookie cutter into the dough, to form about 12 circle shapes, removing the excess.

Transfer to the oven and bake for 30–40 minutes, or until the rounds are firm and golden.

In a bowl, combine the za'atar spice blend with the sumac, if using. Add the olive oil and stir into a paste. Spread about 1 tablespoon of the spice paste over each dough round and bake for a further 5 minutes.

Serve warm, with the cucumber, tomato, gherkins, onion and mint alongside to pile on top, and lemon wedges if desired.

TIP

These breads can be made ahead of time and frozen until needed. Bake the rounds as directed above, but don't spread them with the spice za'atar paste. Leave to cool, then freeze in an airtight container. When you wish to use them, thaw them on the kitchen bench, then spread them with the spice paste and bake in a preheated 180°C (350°F) oven for 4–7 minutes. Serve warm, piled with the toppings.

1 medium-sized head of cauliflower
65 g (2½ oz/½ cup) sorghum flour
2 tablespoons psyllium husks
1 teaspoon onion powder
1 teaspoon garlic powder
¼ teaspoon Himalayan salt
40 g (1½ oz/¼ cup) linseed (flaxseed) meal
45 g (1½ oz/heaped ⅓ cup) za'atar spice blend
½ teaspoon ground sumac (optional)
125 ml (4 fl oz/½ cup) olive oil

To serve
2 Lebanese (short) cucumbers, thinly sliced
2 tomatoes, cut into chunks
4 gherkins (pickles), sliced
1 red onion, cut into thin wedges
a loose handful of mint leaves
lemon wedges (optional)

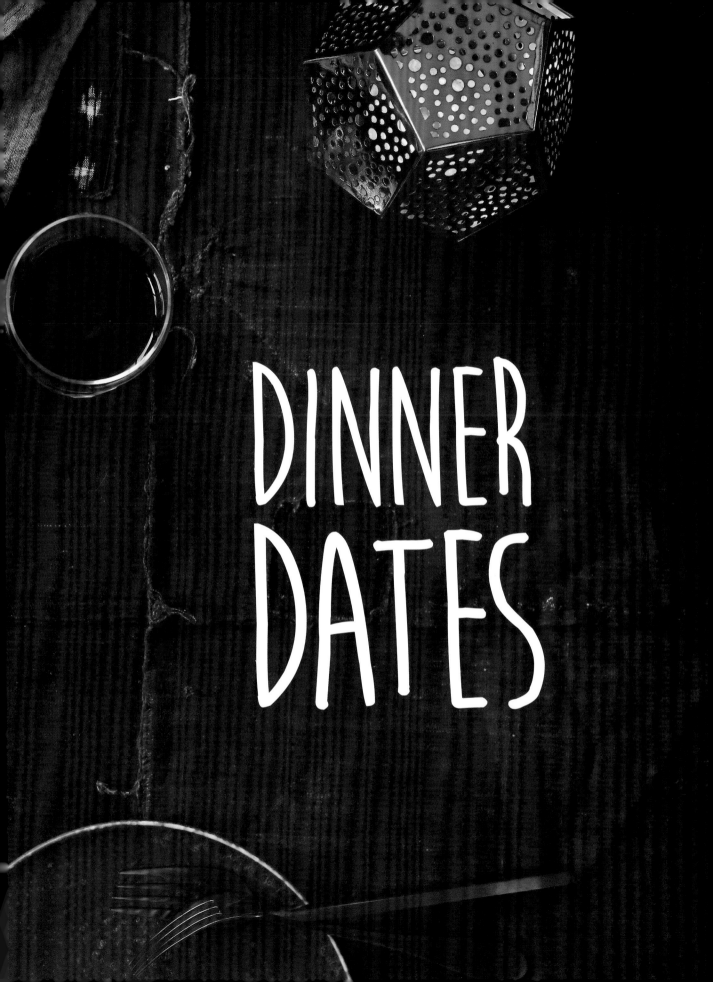

If you're looking for a hearty, nourishing fix, this is your dish. It is rich in protein and fibre, and will have you on a flavour high. As an added bonus, leftovers of the different components will be delicious in salads the next day.

Mediterranean chickpeas with za'atar roasted pumpkin, brown rice & hummus

SERVES 2 ✕ VGN + DF + GF + RSF + NF

Soak the chickpeas in a large bowl of water overnight.

Heat the oil in a saucepan over medium heat. Sauté the onion for 2–3 minutes, or until the onion is translucent. Add the capsicum and sauté for a further 1–2 minutes.

Rinse the chickpeas, add to the saucepan and stir them through.

In a bowl, combine the tomato paste, cumin, salt, pepper and 625 ml (21½ fl oz/2½ cups) water, then pour over the chickpeas. Bring to the boil, cover and reduce the heat to low. Simmer for 25–35 minutes, or until the chickpeas are cooked to your liking; you may need to stir in an extra 1–2 tablespoons water during the cooking process. When the chickpeas are done, keep them warm until serving time.

While the chickpeas are simmering, preheat the oven to 170°C (325°F) and line a baking tray with baking paper, ready to roast the pumpkin.

In a small bowl, combine the za'atar spice blend and olive oil, stirring to create a paste. Massage the spice paste over the pumpkin wedges and place on the lined baking tray. Bake for 25–35 minutes, or until the pumpkin is cooked and golden. Keep warm for serving.

While the pumpkin is in the oven, rinse the rice and cook according to the packet instructions. (Different varieties of rice cook at various rates, so follow the packet directions for the best results.) Keep warm until serving time.

Just before serving, place all the hummus ingredients in a food processor and blend until smooth. Add 2 tablespoons water and continue to whiz until the hummus is smooth and silky.

Serve the warm chickpeas with the rice, roasted pumpkin and hummus, with a side salad of mixed leaves.

TIP If you'd like to use dried chickpeas in the hummus, add an extra 135 g (4¾ oz/⅔ cup) dried chickpeas when preparing the ones for the main dish, then reserve 330 g (11½ oz/2 cups) cooked chickpeas for the hummus.

400 g (14 oz/2 cups) dried chickpeas
1–2 tablespoons olive or grapeseed oil
1 brown onion, finely diced
1 red capsicum (pepper), finely diced
2 heaped tablespoons tomato paste (concentrated purée)
1 heaped teaspoon ground cumin
1 teaspoon Himalayan salt, or to taste
½ teaspoon freshly ground black pepper
625 ml (21½ fl oz/2½ cups) water
220 g (7¾ oz/1 cup) medium-grain brown rice or red rice
50 g (1¾ oz/1 cup) mixed salad leaves

Za'atar roasted pumpkin
1 tablespoon za'atar spice blend
2–3 tablespoons extra virgin olive oil
1 small whole pumpkin (winter squash), cut into wedges

Hummus
330 g (11½ oz/2 cups) cooked or tinned chickpeas, rinsed and drained
3 tablespoons tahini
juice of 1½ lemons
1 garlic clove, crushed
2 tablespoons extra virgin olive oil
½–1 teaspoon Himalayan salt, or to taste

Eggplant parmigiana: Italian comfort food at its best. I have some really special memories that include taste testing this dish when backpacking in Italy as a newlywed. We tasted and we tasted... and fell deeply in love with the simple fusion of fresh flavours. My gosh it's good.

I knew I had to replicate it and I'm so happy with the result. Using cashews as the base for the cheese combines effortlessly with the tomato sauce, pan-fried eggplant and fresh basil to create the magic of this classic Italian dish.

Eggplant parmigiana stack

SERVES 4 ⊗ VGN + DF + GF + RSF

Place the eggplant slices on paper towel and allow to sit for 20 minutes to absorb moisture.

Meanwhile, make a start on the tomato sauce. Heat the olive oil in a saucepan over medium heat and sauté the onion for 1–2 minutes. Add the garlic and stir until fragrant. Stir in the tomatoes, passata, tomato paste and oregano and bring to the boil. Season with the coconut sugar, salt and pepper, then reduce the heat and simmer, uncovered, for 20–30 minutes, stirring occasionally. The sauce should thicken nicely; if you find your sauce is drying out a bit during cooking, stir in a little water. Keep warm until ready to serve.

While the tomato sauce is simmering, finish preparing the eggplant. Heat the olive or coconut oil in a chargrill pan or large frying pan over medium heat. In batches, fry the eggplant slices for 1–2 minutes on each side, or until cooked through (I cover my pan with a lid, to ensure the eggplant cooks through). Set aside and keep warm.

To make the cheesy sauce, drain the pine nuts and cashews, then place in a high-speed food processor. Add the lemon juice and blend until the nuts have broken down into fine pieces. Add the remaining ingredients and process until smooth. (At this point I like to transfer my cheesy sauce to a blender and give it a quick whiz for a smoother, creamier finish, but this is optional.)

When ready to assemble the dish, layer the eggplant on four serving plates, adding a scattering of basil and a drizzle of the tomato sauce and cheesy sauce between each layer.

Serve immediately.

TIP *Before serving, you can place the layered saucy eggplant stack in a baking dish and bake in a preheated 170°C (325°F) oven for 20 minutes. This method cooks the eggplant further, so it almost 'melts' between the sauces.*

2 eggplants (aubergines), sliced about 1 cm (½ inch) thick
1–2 tablespoons olive oil or coconut oil
a handful of basil leaves

Tomato sauce
1 tablespoon olive oil
1 onion, finely diced
1 garlic clove, crushed
400 g (14 oz) tin chopped tomatoes
350 g (12 oz) tomato passata
1 tablespoon tomato paste (concentrated purée)
1 teaspoon chopped oregano leaves
1 tablespoon granulated coconut sugar
½ teaspoon Himalayan salt, or to taste
¼ teaspoon freshly ground black pepper

Cheesy sauce
75 g (2½ oz/½ cup) pine nuts, soaked overnight
75 g (2½ oz/½ cup) cashews, soaked overnight
2 tablespoons lemon juice
2–3 tablespoons almond milk (or more if you prefer a thinner sauce)
2 tablespoons nutritional yeast
½ teaspoon onion powder
½ teaspoon garlic powder
¼ teaspoon Himalayan salt, or to taste

I'm big on making food that appeals to people of all ages. It saves time and effort, and gets children accustomed to eating nourishing 'real' food, rather than nutrient-void 'kid food'.

These tasty little gems pack in some serious nutrition. They are perfect hot or cold, and leftovers taste fabulous with a salad the next day — if, of course, there are any!

You can also make them in advance and freeze them for another day.

Tofu & sweet potato balls

SERVES 8 ✪ VGN + DF + GF + RSF + NF

For the tofu & sweet potato balls

Place the rice and stock in a saucepan and bring to the boil. Cover, reduce the heat and simmer for 20–30 minutes, or until the rice is soft and slightly overcooked. Set aside.

Meanwhile, steam or boil the sweet potato over medium–high heat for 10 minutes, or until just cooked. Set aside.

Heat the grapeseed oil in a frying pan over medium heat and sauté the onion and garlic for about 5 minutes, or until fragrant. Set aside.

Preheat the oven to 170°C (325°F). Line a large baking tray with baking paper.

Place half the sweet potato and half the rice in a food processor. Add half the lentils and half the tofu and process until just combined.

Transfer the mixture to a large bowl. Add the remaining sweet potato, rice, lentils and tofu, along with the peas, tamari, tahini, ginger and curry powder. Using your hands (you may like to pop on some food-handling gloves here), combine well. You want some texture to the mix, so don't over-mash.

Form into round balls, about 2–3 cm (¾–1¼ inches) in diameter, and place on the lined baking tray. (If the mixture is too soft or sticky to roll, chill it in the fridge for about 30 minutes to firm slightly.)

Sprinkle the tofu balls with the sesame seeds and bake for 30–35 minutes, or until golden and cooked through.

Serve the tofu balls warm, with the tomato sauce on the side as a dipping sauce.

For the tomato sauce

Heat the grapeseed oil in a saucepan over medium heat and sauté the onion and chilli for about 5 minutes, or until fragrant. Stir in the tomatoes, maple syrup, vinegar, mustard powder and salt and bring to the boil.

Reduce the heat and simmer, uncovered, for 30–45 minutes, or until the sauce has reduced to a thick paste, stirring occasionally. You may need to stir in a few teaspoons of water during cooking if the sauce is sticking to the pan.

Serve warm, or at room temperature.

Tofu & sweet potato balls

220 g (8 oz/1 cup) medium-grain brown rice, rinsed

500 ml (17 fl oz/2 cups) vegetable stock

300 g (10½ oz/2 cups) peeled, cubed sweet potato

1 tablespoon grapeseed oil

½ brown onion, diced

1 garlic clove, crushed

200 g (7 oz/1 cup) tinned or cooked brown lentils

250 g (9 oz) medium-firm tofu, cut into cubes

75 g (2½ oz/½ cup) fresh or frozen garden peas, cooked

45 ml (1½ fl oz) gluten-free tamari

1 teaspoon tahini

½ teaspoon ground ginger

1–2 teaspoons curry powder

2 tablespoons sesame seeds

Tomato sauce

1–2 teaspoons grapeseed oil

1 large red onion, sliced

1 red chilli, seeded and sliced

500 g (1 lb 2 oz/2 cups) tinned chopped tomatoes

125 ml (4 fl oz/½ cup) maple syrup, or to taste

60 ml (2 fl oz/¼ cup) red wine vinegar

½ teaspoon mustard powder

¼ teaspoon Himalayan salt, or to taste

Grilled corn cobs
with zesty mayo *137*

From top:
Crispy spiced chickpeas *136*

×

Chilli bean nachos *134*

CHILLING WITH FRIENDS

Fun food for you and your crew

Oh nachos, where have you been all my life... Being a late convert to Mexican cuisine, I can honestly cry thinking how many years I've lived without this healthier version of traditional nachos.

This mixture of flavours is pure heaven. The crunchy corn chips dipped in a wholesome tomato chilli bean mix, secret cheezy sauce, cold jalapeño salsa and the perfectly creamy avocado combine flawlessly.

I love my food spicy, so if you prefer it mild, leave out the chilli in the chilli beans and the salsa.

Chilli bean nachos

SERVES 4 ⊗ VGN + DF + GF + RSF

Chilli beans

2 tablespoons olive oil

1 onion, finely diced

2 garlic cloves, crushed

½ jalapeño chilli, sliced

½ red capsicum (pepper), finely diced

400 g (14 oz) tin chopped tomatoes

2 x 425 g (15 oz) tins red kidney beans, rinsed and drained

½ teaspoon ground cumin

¼ teaspoon cayenne pepper

½ teaspoon Himalayan salt, or to taste

⅛ teaspoon freshly ground black pepper

Jalapeño salsa

1 Lebanese (short) cucumber, diced

1 tomato, diced

½ jalapeño chilli, sliced

1 green capsicum (pepper), diced

½ red onion, finely diced

1 tablespoon sliced pitted black olives

2 tablespoons coriander (cilantro) leaves

juice of ½ lemon

⅛ teaspoon Himalayan salt

Secret cheezy sauce

500 g (1 lb 2 oz/4 cups) cauliflower florets, lightly steamed or boiled

125–250 ml (4–9 fl oz/½–1 cup) non-dairy milk

juice of ½ lemon

2 garlic cloves, peeled

3 tablespoons nutritional yeast

½ teaspoon onion powder

½ teaspoon ground turmeric

¼ teaspoon hot paprika

¼ teaspoon Himalayan salt

75 g (2½ oz/½ cup) cashews, soaked for 3–4 hours

1 tablespoon ground yellow maize flour, or 1 tablespoon gluten-free cornflour (cornstarch)

Chunky avo

2 ripe avocados

juice of 1–2 limes

1 garlic clove, crushed

¼ teaspoon Himalayan salt, or to taste

To serve

75 g (2½ oz/2 cups) organic non-GMO corn chips

lime cheeks or wedges

For the chilli beans

Heat the olive oil in a saucepan over medium heat. Add the onion and sauté for 3–4 minutes, or until the onion is tender. Stir in the garlic and cook for 30 seconds.

Add the jalapeño chilli and capsicum and sauté for a further 1–2 minutes, or until fragrant. Stir in the tomatoes and bring to the boil.

Add the remaining ingredients and stir to combine. Bring back to the boil, then reduce the heat and simmer, uncovered, for 15–20 minutes, to bring all the flavours together. You may need to add 1–2 tablespoons water if your mixture is looking thick.

The chilli beans could be made a day or two ahead; keep in the fridge in an airtight container and gently reheat just before serving.

For the jalapeño salsa

Near serving time, combine all the ingredients in a bowl. Cover and set aside.

For the secret cheezy sauce

When you're nearly ready to serve, place the cauliflower in a food processor or blender with the milk and lemon juice and blend until smooth.

Add the garlic, nutritional yeast, onion powder, turmeric, paprika and salt and blend until you have a thick and creamy sauce.

Add the cashews and maize flour and blend until completely smooth.

For the chunky avo

Just before serving, remove the stones from the avocados. Scoop the flesh of one avocado into a bowl and roughly mash with a fork. Add the lime juice, garlic and salt and mash until well combined.

Dice the other avocado into chunky pieces and gently mix through the mashed avocado. You should have some smooth and chunky pieces.

Assembling the nachos

Arrange the corn chips, chilli beans, cheezy sauce, chunky avo and jalapeño salsa in a bowl. Add some lime cheeks or wedges.

Take a corn chip, top with some beans and a bit of each condiment and devour!

Seriously tasty, these spiced chickpeas make a crunchy and nutritious addition to your savoury meals. They also make a perfect snack and keep really well, so you can make a big batch and munch on them for weeks!

Chickpeas are a low-kilojoule wholefood boasting high levels of iron, zinc, phosphorus, folate and other B vitamins, all of which are especially important for vegetarians and vegans. Full of fibre and satisfying protein, they also help curb hunger pangs.

Crispy spiced chickpeas

SERVES 2–4 ⊗ VGN + DF + GF + RSF + NF

Preheat the oven to 180°C (350°F). Line a baking tray with baking paper.

Drain and thoroughly dry the chickpeas with a tea towel.

Toss the chickpeas in the coconut oil to lightly coat, then spread them out on the baking tray. Bake for 40–50 minutes, or until crunchy, tossing a few times during cooking to ensure even baking. Remove from the oven.

While still warm, evenly coat the chickpeas with the spices. (I like to place the spices in a fine-mesh sieve and sift them over the chickpeas, giving them a quick toss to lightly coat all over.)

Enjoy the chickpeas on their own, straight out of the oven, or leave to cool completely and save for snacking on or adding to salads and soups. The chickpeas will keep in an airtight container in the pantry for several weeks.

400 g (14 oz/2 cups) dried chickpeas, soaked in water overnight
1 tablespoon melted coconut oil
½ teaspoon garlic powder
¼ teaspoon onion powder
¼ teaspoon curry powder
⅛ teaspoon Himalayan salt
⅛ teaspoon hot paprika

These luscious grilled cobs drizzled with a zesty mayo bring out the greed in us: we can never cook up enough cobs to satisfy our cravings. When it's time to serve these and our other favourite side dish, the Chunky sweet potato chips (page 150), it's almost fight night at our place.

When choosing your corn, for the best flavour, look for the freshest organic, locally grown, non-genetically modified corn and avoid the imported varieties.

Grilled corn cobs with zesty mayo

SERVES 4 ✪ VGN + DF + GF + RSF

Remove the thick outer layers from each corn husk; this is usually the outer two or three layers. Peel back the thin, inner husk layers, but do not remove them — the corn cobs will look and taste better after grilling!

Remove the silks from the husks, just by pulling them out. (The silks are the fine, string-like pieces that poke out from under the husk, near the top of the cob.)

Soak the cobs in water for 15–20 minutes, to stop them drying out during grilling. Meanwhile, heat a barbecue or chargrill pan to medium heat.

Drain the corn cobs and dry them thoroughly. Peel back the husks and brush the corn kernels with the olive oil. Allow the husks to return to their natural position, fully covering the kernels.

Grill the corn cobs for 15 minutes, turning often to evenly cook each side. You will notice the husks developing grill marks.

Reduce the heat to low. Peel back the husks to expose the kernels, then grill for a further 15 minutes, turning often.

Meanwhile, make the zesty mayo (see tip). Drain the cashews

and place in a food processor or high-speed blender. Add the olive oil and 60 ml (2 fl oz/¼ cup) water and process until smooth. Add the remaining mayo ingredients and process until smooth, adding a little more water if needed.

When the corn is ready, remove from the heat. Peel the husks back, then drizzle the mayo over the cobs. Garnish with the coriander, lime zest, and chopped chilli if desired. Eat while hot.

TIP I often double the zesty mayo recipe so there are enough ingredients in my food processor for the blades to circle well and beat everything together for a smooth result; the leftover mayo will keep in the fridge for several days and can be used to accompany a host of other dishes, such as the Roast garlic & rosemary potato chips (page 144), or instead of the aioli with the Chunky sweet potato chips (page 150). Another option is to blend up the quantity noted in the recipe using a processor, then quickly blitz in a high-speed blender for a really smooth finish.

4 fresh ears of corn, with husks
2 teaspoons olive oil
a handful of chopped coriander (cilantro)
grated zest of ½ lime
1 red chilli, finely sliced (optional)

Zesty mayo
150 g (5½ oz/1 cup) cashews, soaked overnight
1 tablespoon olive oil
flesh of ½ avocado
juice of 2 limes
grated zest of ½ lime
½ cup coriander (cilantro) leaves
2 garlic cloves, peeled
¼–½ teaspoon chilli powder
¼ teaspoon Himalayan salt
⅛ teaspoon freshly ground black pepper

A hearty dish recalling all those wonderful bolognese flavours, except this version is fully plant based. When I need a warming, satisfying comfort meal, it gives me all those feel-good sensations: it reminds me of my early days, when rich tomato-based bolognese was on our weekly Monday night menu, making Monday my favourite night of the week! Now I offer this nourishing version to my own children every Monday, and they wouldn't have it any other way.

Lentil bolognese with zucchini noodles

SERVES 4 ✪ VGN + DF + GF + RSF + NF

Drain and rinse the lentils; set aside.

Heat the oil in a large saucepan over medium heat. Add the onion and sauté for 2–3 minutes, or until translucent. Add the garlic and stir until fragrant.

Add the carrot and mushrooms and stir through for a minute or two.

Mix the lentils through.

Combine the tomato paste, salt, pepper and 375 ml (13 fl oz/ 1½ cups) water, then pour over the lentil mixture. Stir in the passata until well combined and bring to the boil.

Add the whole basil bunch, reduce the heat to a simmer, then cover and cook for 25–30 minutes. Remove the bunch of basil and check the sauce; you may want to stir in a little more water if the sauce is thickening too quickly.

Put the lid back on and simmer for a further 20–30 minutes, or until the sauce is cooked to your liking. Keep warm.

Using a spiraliser or vegetable peeler, create 'noodles' from the zucchini and transfer to one large serving bowl, or four individual bowls.

Pour the lentil bolognese sauce over the zucchini noodles. Garnish with extra basil leaves, sprinkle with chilli flakes if desired, and enjoy straightaway.

Leftovers can be frozen in an airtight container for up to 4 weeks.

TIP *You can make the bolognese ahead of time and freeze any leftovers. It's always a wonderful surprise finding it in your freezer on those days when you're feeling time poor.*

430 g (15½ oz/2 cups) dried green lentils, soaked for 8–10 hours

2 tablespoons grapeseed or olive oil

1 onion, finely diced

3 garlic cloves, crushed

1 carrot, finely grated

100 g (3½ oz) brown mushrooms, halved

1 tablespoon tomato paste (concentrated purée)

½ teaspoon sea salt, or to taste

¼ teaspoon freshly cracked black pepper

700 g (1 lb 9 oz) tomato passata

1 bunch (125 g/4½ oz) fresh basil, tied with string, plus extra basil leaves to serve

4 zucchini (courgettes)

1 tablespoon chilli flakes (optional)

CREATE HEALTHY HABITS, NOT RESTRICTIONS

Nourish bowls are a bit of an addiction. I'll go one for lunch or dinner, with various vegie combinations. Made to be shared, this nourish platter is definitely a favourite. Lentils are a vegetarian's dream, and are ideal combined with quinoa, thrown together in zesty salads and served with roasted vegies. These cumin-spiced lentils really star among all the other fresh plant-based ingredients.

Enjoy the nourishment this platter offers. Include it in your weekly lunch list and let it become a staple for you too.

Lentil nourish platter

SERVES 4 ✪ VGN + DF + GF + RSF + NF

Rinse the lentils and place in a saucepan with 500 ml (17 fl oz/ 2 cups) water. Bring to the boil. Stir in the cumin, paprika, salt and pepper, then reduce the heat, cover and simmer for 10–25 minutes, or until the lentils are just tender.

Meanwhile, place the quinoa and stock in a saucepan and bring to the boil. Cover with lid and simmer for 10 minutes, or until cooked.

Heat the olive oil in a frying pan over medium heat. Add the onion and cook, stirring often, for about 5 minutes. Reduce the heat to low and cook for a further 5 minutes, or until the onion is caramelised, stirring regularly so it doesn't burn. Remove from the heat.

In a small bowl, combine the dressing ingredients.

Arrange the quinoa, lentils and caramelised onion in small mounds on a platter. Add the cucumber, fennel, tomatoes and mixed leaves. Top with the dill, mint and parsley. Drizzle with the dressing and serve immediately, with the garlic dip.

215 g (7½ oz/1 cup) dried green lentils, soaked for 8–10 hours
1½ teaspoons ground cumin
½ teaspoon hot paprika
½ teaspoon Himalayan salt, or to taste
¼ teaspoon freshly cracked black pepper
200 g (7 oz/1 cup) quinoa, rinsed
375 ml (13 fl oz/1½ cups) vegetable stock
1–2 tablespoons olive oil
1 large brown onion, thinly sliced
2 Lebanese (short) cucumbers, cut into ribbons using a mandoline or vegetable peeler
1 fennel bulb, thinly sliced
150 g (5½ oz/1 cup) cherry tomatoes, halved
50 g (1¾ oz/1 cup) mixed salad leaves
a handful of dill sprigs
25 g (1 oz/½ cup) finely chopped mint
15 g (½ oz/½ cup) finely chopped flat-leaf (Italian) parsley
1 generous tablespoon vegan nut-free garlic dip

Dressing
60 ml (2 fl oz/¼ cup) extra virgin olive oil
juice of 1 lemon
1 garlic clove, crushed
½–1 teaspoon sumac
¼ teaspoon Himalayan salt
⅛ teaspoon freshly cracked black pepper

Crispy on the outside, soft on the inside, hot potato chips are my weakness! Potatoes are often given a bad rap because many people deep-fry them or mash them with butter and cream — but take away the excess oil and roast potatoes are a low-calorie, high-fibre food that tastes too good to live without.

All hail kale! This recipe is awesome. The ideal side dish or snack, it packs a punch in the nutritional department and tastes amazing. I've tried lots of flavour combinations for kale chips and enjoy them in lots of ways, but this one is definitely a fave. Give it a go and fall in love with this superfood. It's also a great way to get your kids into kale — just skip the chilli.

Roast garlic & rosemary potato chips

SERVES 4 ✪ VGN + DF + GF + RSF + NF

4 red-skinned potatoes, about 600 g (1 lb 5 oz) in total, cut into long chip shapes 1 cm (¾ inch) thick
1 tablespoon olive oil
2–3 garlic cloves, crushed
1 rosemary sprig, chopped
¼ teaspoon Himalayan salt

Preheat the oven to 180°C (350°F). Line a baking tray with baking paper.

Bring a large saucepan of water to the boil. Add the potato slices, allow to boil for a couple of minutes, then drain. You don't want the potatoes to cook through at this point, so 1–2 minutes is enough boiling time.

Pat the potatoes dry using a clean tea towel.

In a small bowl, combine the olive oil, garlic, rosemary and salt.

Massage the oil mixture over the potato slices, then spread them out on the baking tray. Bake for 30–40 minutes, or until cooked through and crispy, tossing halfway through cooking to ensure even baking.

Serve hot, with a small bowl of smashed avocado for dipping into, or as a side dish to the Eggplant parmigiana on page 128 and see how quickly they disappear!

Crispy kale chips

SERVES 2 ✪ VGN + DF + GF + RSF + NF

280 g (10 oz/4 cups, firmly packed) curly kale leaves, stems removed, leaves torn into large pieces
1 tablespoon melted coconut oil
1 tablespoon nutritional yeast
½ teaspoon onion powder
½ teaspoon garlic powder
¼–½ teaspoon chilli powder
⅛ teaspoon Himalayan salt, or to taste

Preheat the oven to 160°C (315°F). Line two large baking trays with baking paper.

Rinse the kale leaves and dry them thoroughly.

Combine the remaining ingredients in a bowl.

Massage the mixture over the kale and spread the leaves evenly on the baking trays, ensuring the leaves do not overlap.

Bake for 15 minutes, or until the kale is cooked, browned and crispy. You may like to toss the leaves over halfway through cooking to ensure they are baking evenly.

Remove from the oven and leave to rest for 3–5 minutes before serving, to let the kale chips become extra crispy.

Serve straightaway.

Miso eggplant *148*

✕

Spicy sesame edamame *151*

SOMETHING ON THE SIDE
Making sides a stand-out

Cauliflower
cheese 149

×

Chunky sweet potato
chips with aioli 150

Japanese cuisine is a huge family favourite; we get serious withdrawals if we miss our weekly session at our local restaurant. Here's a spin on one of the classics, in which the eggplant is lightly pan-fried, glazed with a miso paste, then baked to perfection in the oven. Not your typical deep-fried method, but amazing nonetheless.

Eggplant can be a bit tricky to work with. If you don't use enough oil, you tend to get a rubbery or half-cooked result: it's a fine line between using too little and just enough. This recipe should help you reach the desired outcome, without needing to use too much oil.

Miso eggplant

SERVES 4 ✗ VGN + DF + GF + RSF + NF

Preheat the oven to 170°C (325°F). Line a baking tray with baking paper.

Cut each eggplant in half lengthways. Using a sharp knife, score the inside in squares about 2.5 cm (1 inch) deep.

Add half the grapeseed oil to a large frying pan set over medium–high heat. Working in batches, add the eggplant halves, skin facing down, and cook for 2–3 minutes, or until the skin is browned.

Turn the eggplant over and cover with a lid. Fry the eggplant for 3–4 minutes, or more, until the eggplant is cooked through. You may need to add a little more oil in the process.

In a bowl, combine the tahini, vinegar, miso paste, maple syrup, sesame oil and 60 ml (2 fl oz/¼ cup) water. Mix together well.

Spoon the miso mixture over the scored side of each eggplant half. Place them on the baking tray, with the scored side facing up. Transfer to the oven and bake for 5–6 minutes, or until the miso mixture is lightly bubbling.

Sprinkle with the sesame seeds, garnish with the spring onion and serve.

4 eggplants (aubergines)
45–60 ml (1½–2 fl oz) grapeseed oil
1 tablespoon tahini
1 tablespoon rice vinegar
2 tablespoons miso paste
1–2 teaspoons maple syrup
1 teaspoon sesame oil
2 tablespoons sesame seeds, lightly toasted
1 tablespoon chopped spring onion (scallion)

Some things are just too good to live without. Cauliflower cheese is one of them. Here it's given a healthy dose of colour and yum with the addition of broccoli and a no-cheese cheese. Yep, that's right: a super-simple version involving a no-cheese sauce that tastes very, well, cheesy.

As cruciferous vegetables, broccoli and cauliflower are among the healthiest things you can eat — and when cooked right, they taste awesome. This comforting combo makes a regular appearance on our dinner table.

Cauliflower cheese

SERVES 4 ⊗ VGN + DF + GF + RSF + NF

Preheat the oven to 180°C (350°F).

Place the broccoli and cauliflower in a large mixing bowl.

Mix together the grapeseed oil, onion powder, garlic powder and paprika, then pour over the broccoli and cauliflower.

Transfer to a baking dish and bake for 25–30 minutes, or until the vegies are tender and browned.

Combine the no-cheese sauce ingredients and pour over the broccoli and cauliflower. Return to the oven for about 5 minutes to brown further.

Serve hot.

TIP *Almond milk also tastes lovely in this recipe instead of coconut milk, if nut products are not a problem in your family.*

350 g (12 oz) broccoli, cut into florets
350 g (12 oz) cauliflower, cut into florets
1 tablespoon grapeseed oil
½ teaspoon onion powder
½ teaspoon garlic powder
¼ teaspoon hot paprika

No-cheese sauce
185 ml (6 fl oz/¾ cup) coconut milk
1 tablespoon tahini
3 tablespoons nutritional yeast
½ teaspoon Himalayan salt
¼ teaspoon freshly ground black pepper

Chunky chips straight out of the oven could possibly be my favourite food ever — and I'm probably not alone in that. I like mine baked, then served with a creamy dipping sauce, and this combination hits the spot.

Sweet potatoes are high in vitamin A, and studies suggest that eating more plant foods such as these decreases the risk of obesity, diabetes and heart disease, while also promoting a healthy complexion, increased energy and overall lower weight. Thank you sweet potato.

Chunky sweet potato chips with aioli

SERVES 2 ⊗ VGN + DF + GF + RSF

Preheat the oven to 180°C (350°F).

Combine the coconut flour, potato flour, salt, garlic powder, paprika and cumin in a bowl.

Lightly brush each sweet potato chip with the coconut oil. Lightly sprinkle each chip with the flour mixture. You don't want a heavy coating of oil or flour, so be sure to use a light hand. (Once I've oiled the chips, I place the spiced flour mixture in a fine-mesh sieve and sift it over the chips for an even and light distribution.)

Place the chips on a baking tray, with space between each chip. Bake for 35–40 minutes, or until cooked and crispy, tossing the chips halfway through to ensure even baking.

Serve hot, with the aioli.

For the aioli

Drain the cashews and place in a blender with the lemon juice, vinegar, salt and 125 ml (4 fl oz/½ cup) water. Whiz until smooth.

Add the garlic and blend briefly, then blend in the mustard.

Gradually add the olive oil, continuing to blend until the mixture is super smooth; you may need to add a little extra water if it's too thick.

The aioli can be made a day ahead if required and kept covered in the fridge; bring to room temperature for serving.

1 tablespoon coconut flour
1 tablespoon potato flour
½ teaspoon Himalayan salt, or to taste
½ teaspoon garlic powder
¼ teaspoon hot paprika
¼ teaspoon ground cumin
1 orange sweet potato, skin left on, cut into chunky chips
1 tablespoon melted coconut oil

Aioli
150 g (5½ oz/1 cup) cashews, soaked overnight
45 ml (1½ fl oz) lemon juice
1 tablespoon apple cider vinegar
¼ teaspoon Himalayan salt, or to taste
2 garlic cloves, peeled
1 teaspoon dijon or wholegrain mustard
60–125 ml (2–4 fl oz/¼–½ cup) mild-tasting olive oil

Sometimes the simple things are the best:
like my spicy sesame edamame.
These addictive little soy beans are our
favourite family snack. My kids like them
fresh, hot and lightly salted, but my husband
and I like to heat things up with a kick of chilli.
Super easy, and full of fibre, healthy fats
and protein, these spicy sesame edamame
will soon have you hooked.

Spicy sesame edamame

SERVES 4 ⊗ VGN + DF + GF + RSF + NF

400 g (14 oz) frozen edamame (green soy beans),
   in their pods
½–1 teaspoon Himalayan salt flakes
½ teaspoon garlic powder
¼ teaspoon chilli powder
¼ teaspoon chilli flakes
1 teaspoon sesame oil

Bring a large saucepan of water to the boil. Add the
edamame and allow to boil for just 1 minute. (Frozen
edamame are already cooked, so you're just revitalising
them in this step.) Drain, pat dry with a clean tea towel
and set aside.

Place the salt, garlic powder, chilli powder and chilli
flakes in a dry frying pan over medium heat. Lightly toast
for 2–3 minutes, or until fragrant, stirring them so they
don't burn.

Drizzle the edamame with the sesame oil and gently
toss to coat. Add them to the spices in the frying pan
and mix until evenly coated.

Serve hot, straight out of the pan.

My parents loved cooking, so our family meals were full of flavour, passion and tradition. Falafel was a household favourite, and this healthy baked version is as tasty as it gets. The best thing is that you don't need to use a deep-fryer. The tabouleh, made with quinoa instead of cracked wheat, is gluten free, with pomegranate seeds adding zest. Drizzle with tahini sauce for a match made in heaven.

Baked falafels with quinoa tabouleh & tahini sauce

SERVES 4 ✷ VGN + DF + GF + RSF + NF

For the falafels

Preheat the oven to 170°C (325°F). Line a baking tray with baking paper.

In a small saucepan, bring the quinoa and 185 ml (6 fl oz/¾ cup) water to the boil over medium–high heat. Cover, reduce the heat and simmer for 5–8 minutes, or until just cooked. Remove from the heat and allow to cool.

Rinse the chickpeas, then pulse in a food processor until broken down into small crumbs. Add the quinoa, garlic, onion, parsley and coriander and process until well combined.

Transfer the mixture to a bowl and add the remaining falafel ingredients. Mix together well. Using your hands (you may want to slip on some food-handling gloves), roll the mixture into 8–10 small balls, the size of golf balls. Gently flatten the tops, into a dome shape.

Place on the lined baking tray and bake for 40–45 minutes, or until golden and cooked through.

The falafels are best served immediately. They can be stored in the fridge and gently reheated, but won't be as tasty.

For the quinoa tabouleh

In a small saucepan, bring the quinoa and 125 ml (4 fl oz/½ cup) water to the boil over medium–high heat. Cover, reduce the heat and simmer for 5 minutes. Remove from the heat and allow to cool.

Place the quinoa in a large bowl. Add the tomatoes, parsley, spring onion, mint and pomegranate seeds.

In a small bowl, whisk together the olive oil, lemon juice and salt, adding the chilli if you like extra kick. Drizzle over the tabouleh and toss together.

For the tahini sauce

In a bowl, vigorously whisk the tahini and 125 ml (4 fl oz/½ cup) water with a fork. Whisk in the garlic, lemon juice, salt and paprika, if using.

To serve

Serve the falafels and tabouleh with the tahini sauce for drizzling over, with your choice of accompaniments.

TIP You'll need two lots of quinoa, for the falafels and the tabouleh, so cook it all up at the same time. Simmer 150 g (5½ oz/¾ cup) quinoa in 310 ml (10¾ fl oz/1¼ cups) water; use two-thirds in the falafels, and the rest in the tabouleh.

Falafels

100 g (3½ oz/½ cup) quinoa, rinsed (see tip)

200 g (7 oz/1 cup) dried chickpeas, soaked in cold water for 8–10 hours

5 garlic cloves, peeled

2 large brown onions, roughly chopped

1 bunch flat-leaf (Italian) parsley, stems removed, to give 20 g (1 oz/1 cup) picked leaves

1 bunch coriander (cilantro), stems removed, to give 15 g (½ oz/½ cup) picked leaves

2 tablespoons sesame seeds

¾ teaspoon ground cumin

½ teaspoon Himalayan salt

¼ teaspoon freshly ground black pepper

¼ teaspoon hot paprika

1 teaspoon bicarbonate of soda (baking soda)

Quinoa tabouleh

50 g (1¾ oz/¼ cup) quinoa, rinsed (see Tip)

125 ml (4 fl oz/½ cup) water

3 tomatoes, diced

2 bunches flat-leaf (Italian) parsley, leaves picked, to give 60 g (2¼ oz/ 2 cups) finely chopped leaves

3 spring onions (scallions), chopped

½ bunch mint, stems removed, to give 25 g (1 oz/½ cup) finely chopped leaves

60 g (2¼ oz/⅓ cup) pomegranate seeds

60 ml (2 fl oz/¼ cup) extra virgin olive oil

juice of 3 lemons

¼ teaspoon Himalayan salt, or to taste

½ red chilli (optional), finely chopped

Tahini sauce

125 g (4½ oz/½ cup) tahini

1 garlic clove, crushed

juice of 1 lemon

¼ teaspoon Himalayan salt, or to taste

¼ teaspoon hot paprika (optional)

To serve

1 long red chilli, sliced (optional)

cornichons or small gherkins (optional)

iceberg lettuce cups, or gluten-free flat breads

If there's one thing we can rely on, it's spaghetti with a classic homemade tomato sauce. It's comfort food at its very best, and when made with fresh healthy ingredients, there's no reason why you can't enjoy it regularly.

Here you have my vegie-packed version of the beloved Italian-style sauce. This one's a weekly favourite at our place. Easy to prepare and delicious to eat, we can't get enough of it.

Classic tomato spaghetti

SERVES 6 ⊗ VGN + DF + GF + RSF + NF

Heat the olive oil in a saucepan over medium heat. Add the onion and cook, stirring, for 2–3 minutes. Add the garlic and stir until fragrant.

Stir the carrot and zucchini through. Stir in the passata, tomato paste and 250 ml (9 fl oz/1 cup) water and bring to the boil.

Add the mushrooms and basil bunch and season with the salt and pepper. Reduce the heat and simmer, uncovered, for 30 minutes, stirring occasionally.

Remove the basil bunch and simmer for a further 30 minutes, stirring occasionally.

When the sauce is nearly ready, cook the pasta according to the packet directions.

Drain the pasta and add to a large saucepan with 500 g (1 lb 2 oz/ 2 cups) of the spaghetti sauce; freeze the remaining sauce to use another day. Stir until the spaghetti has reached your desired temperature.

Divide the spaghetti among serving bowls. Drizzle with the extra virgin olive oil and sprinkle with the chilli flakes, if using. Garnish with extra basil leaves and serve.

500 g (1 lb 2 oz) gluten-free spaghetti, preferably wholegrain

Tomato sauce
1 tablespoon olive oil
1 onion, finely diced
3 garlic cloves, crushed
1 carrot, finely grated
1 zucchini (courgette), finely grated
700 g (1 lb 9 oz) tomato passata
2 tablespoons tomato paste (concentrated purée)
100 g (3½ oz) Swiss brown mushrooms (I leave mine whole)
1 bunch (125 g/4½ oz) fresh basil, tied with string, plus extra basil leaves to serve
1 teaspoon sea salt, or to taste
½ teaspoon freshly ground black pepper
1 tablespoon extra virgin olive oil
1 teaspoon chilli flakes (optional)

I'm a fan of stuffed anything. I'm always on the lookout for any new vegetable that I can stuff... literally! It must be my mum's influence as she used to make stuffed eggplant, capsicum and zucchini for us all the time.

This stuffed capsicum dish isn't based on my mum's traditional recipe, but is a ripper vegie variation. Quinoa is always in fashion with me, and plays the star role in the stuffing, alongside a medley of vegetables and spices that make this dish a taste bomb.

Stuffed capsicums

SERVES 4 ✪ VGN + DF + GF + RSF + NF

Preheat the oven to 170°C (325°F). Place the capsicum halves on a baking tray lined with baking paper and lightly massage with 1 teaspoon olive oil.

Put the quinoa and 625 ml (21½ fl oz/2½ cups) vegetable stock in a saucepan and bring to the boil. Reduce the heat, cover and simmer for 10–12 minutes, or until the stock is absorbed and the quinoa is cooked. Set aside to cool slightly.

Mix the 125 ml (4½ fl oz/½ cup) vegetable stock with the tomato paste and set aside.

Heat the grapeseed oil in a saucepan over medium heat. Sauté the onion for 2–3 minutes, or until translucent. Add the garlic and chilli and sauté for a further 1–2 minutes.

Stir in the diced tomatoes, then add the tomato paste mixture, salt, pepper, basil and the 15 g (½ oz/¼ cup) nutritional yeast. Remove from the heat when the mixture begins to bubble.

In a large bowl, combine the corn, peas, black beans and quinoa. Add the tomato mixture and fold through well.

Evenly scoop the mixture into the capsicum halves. Drizzle with a little extra olive oil, then transfer to the oven and bake for 15 minutes.

Sprinkle the extra nutritional yeast over the capsicum halves and bake for a further 10–20 minutes, or until cooked to your liking.

Transfer to a serving platter and enjoy straightaway.

4 capsicums (peppers), in a mix of colours, cut in half lengthways, then hollowed out

1 teaspoon olive oil, plus extra for drizzling

300 g (10½ oz/1½ cups) quinoa

625 ml (21½ fl oz/2½ cups) vegetable stock, plus an extra 125 ml (4½ fl oz/½ cup) vegetable stock

1 tablespoon tomato paste (concentrated purée)

2 tablespoons grapeseed oil

1 red onion, finely diced

3 garlic cloves, crushed

1 long red chilli, diced (optional)

2 ripe tomatoes, peeled and diced

1 teaspoon Himalayan salt, or to taste

½ teaspoon freshly ground black pepper

½ teaspoon dried basil

15 g (½ oz/¼ cup) nutritional yeast, plus an extra 2 tablespoons for sprinkling

200 g (7 oz/1 cup) cooked corn kernels

75 g (1½ oz/½ cup) cooked fresh or frozen peas

175 g (6 oz/1 cup) cooked or tinned black beans, rinsed and drained

SWEET
FIX

Familiar tastes and associated memories play a major role in my recipe development. These jam biscuits remind me of a childhood favourite, and fit into the 'hard to believe they are healthy' category.

With this version you have strawberry chia jam and a smooth coconut-cream spread sandwiched between two crumbly, perfectly baked oat cookies, for a delectable morning or afternoon-tea treat. Even my sugar-obsessed dad gave them a thumbs up. A winner.

Jam biscuit sandwiches

MAKES 8 ✖ VGN + DF + GF + RSF

For the biscuits

Preheat the oven to 160°C (315°F). Line a baking tray with baking paper.

Combine the oats, coconut, coconut sugar, vanilla, baking powder and salt in a bowl. Add the coconut oil and almond butter and mix well, using your hands.

In a cup, mix the linseed meal and 45 ml (1½ fl oz) water. Place in the fridge for 5–10 minutes, or until the mixture gels together and takes on an egg-white consistency.

It's helpful to pop on some food-handling gloves here. Add the linseed mixture to the oat mixture and mix in until well incorporated.

Roll the mixture into 16 small balls, about 2–3 cm (¾–1¼ inches) in diameter, and place on the baking tray; there is no need to press them down, as the biscuits will flatten in the oven. Bake for 20–25 minutes, or until the biscuits have browned.

Leave to cool completely before filling. The unfilled biscuits will keep in an airtight container in the pantry for 2–3 days.

For the chia jam

Place the strawberries, rice malt syrup and vanilla in a blender and process until smooth. Transfer to a bowl and stir in the chia seeds. Place in the fridge for up to 30 minutes to set.

For the creme

Put the cashews and 60 ml (2 fl oz/ ¼ cup) water in a high-speed blender or food processor and blend until smooth (see tip).

Place the cashew mixture in a small bowl. Scoop 2 tablespoons of hardened coconut cream (from the top part of the tin) into the bowl. Add the cacao butter, rice malt syrup and vanilla and mix until well combined.

Assembling the biscuits

Spread a teaspoon of the creme and a teaspoon of chia jam on the underside of half the biscuits. Place another biscuit on top. The biscuits will keep in the fridge for 1–2 days.

TIP When making the creme using a large processor or blender, you may find it hard to get a proper blend due to the small quantity. If so, you can double the ingredients to get your machine moving, then use half the creme mixture now, and freeze the rest in a small airtight container for next time; it will keep in the freezer for up to 4 weeks.

Biscuits

180 g (6 oz/2 cups) gluten-free rolled (porridge) oats, ground to a flour in a food processor

45 g (1½ oz/½ cup) desiccated coconut

100 g (3½ oz/½ cup) granulated coconut sugar

½ teaspoon vanilla powder

½ teaspoon gluten-free baking powder

⅛ teaspoon Himalayan salt

125 ml (4 fl oz/½ cup) melted coconut oil

2 tablespoons almond butter

1 tablespoon linseed (flaxseed) meal

Chia jam

200 g (7 oz) strawberries, chopped

2 tablespoons rice malt syrup

¼ teaspoon vanilla powder

2 tablespoons white chia seeds

Creme

75 g (2½ oz/½ cup) cashews, soaked for 6–8 hours

2 tablespoons coconut cream (from a tin of coconut cream that has been refrigerated overnight)

2 tablespoons melted cacao butter

1 tablespoon rice malt syrup

½ teaspoon natural vanilla extract

I'm still cartwheeling over this beauty. It wasn't the easiest recipe to develop — it took countless attempts over eight or nine months to get it right! — but it is one of my most satisfying, as the biscuit, jam, marshmallow and chocolate elements all combine effortlessly to deliver a serious taste high. A delicious treat at any time, for any occasion. You have to try it to believe it.

Cartwheels

MAKES 5 ⊗ R + VGN + DF + GF + RSF + NF

To make the biscuits, put the buckwheat groats in a food processor and blitz into small crumbs. Add the coconut and process until well combined. Add the dates and process until sticky and well combined.

Transfer the mixture to a cutting board, then roll it out so it is only about 2 mm (1/16 inch) thick.

Use a 6 cm (2½ inch) round cookie cutter to cut out 10 cookie shapes from the dough. Place them on a plate lined with baking paper and transfer to the freezer while making the chia jam.

Make the jam by processing the strawberries in a food processor or blender. Add the rice malt syrup and vanilla and process until well combined. Spoon the strawberry mixture into a bowl and stir the chia seeds through. Place in the fridge to set for 15 minutes or so.

Once the jam has set, remove the biscuits from the freezer and spread a thin layer over five of the biscuits. Freeze for at least another 3–4 hours.

To make the marshmallow layer, put the coconut butter in a bowl, add 2 tablespoons of boiling water and stir until softened together.

Scrape 2 tablespoons of hardened coconut cream from the top of the tin and add to the coconut butter. Add the rice malt syrup, vanilla and marshmallow oil and stir together, until the mixture is firm but velvety. Set aside.

To make the chocolate, combine the cacao butter and coconut oil in a bowl. Stir in the cacao powder. Add the maple syrup and stir well until the mixture is thick and glossy. If the chocolate is runny, transfer to the fridge for up to 15 minutes to thicken slightly.

Place a sheet of baking paper on the kitchen bench, then set a wire baking rack on top. Remove the biscuits from the freezer. Slather the marshmallow mixture over five of the biscuits and sandwich the other biscuits on top.

Dip the biscuits into the chocolate and set on the wire racks to catch the drips. Depending on the thickness of your chocolate, you may need to double coat them.

Once they have all been coated, set the biscuits in the fridge for 10 minutes before serving.

The biscuits will keep in an airtight container in the freezer for 6–8 weeks.

Biscuits
140 g (4 oz/¾ cup) activated buckwheat groats
35 g (1¼ oz/½ cup) shredded coconut
8–10 medjool dates, pitted

Chia jam
200 g (7 oz) strawberries, hulled and chopped
2 tablespoons rice malt syrup
¼ teaspoon vanilla powder
2 tablespoons white chia seeds

Marshmallow
2–3 tablespoons softened coconut butter
2 tablespoons coconut cream (from a tin of coconut cream that has been refrigerated overnight)
1 tablespoon rice malt syrup
¼ teaspoon natural vanilla extract
¼ teaspoon natural marshmallow-flavoured oil, such as LorAnn (optional)

Chocolate
60 ml (2 fl oz/¼ cup) melted cacao butter
60 ml (2 fl oz/¼ cup) melted coconut oil
85 g (3 oz/¾ cup) raw cacao powder
60 ml (2 fl oz/¼ cup) maple syrup

Cherry and chocolate — I'm in love. You won't be able to keep your hands off these babies, made with a combination of dried cherries, coconut, cacao powder and creamy nut butter, then coated in homemade chocolate. A densely satisfying sweet and sour sensation, perfect for when you get that chocolate craving.

Cherry bites

MAKES 12 ✪ R + VGN + DF + GF + RSF

Place the dried cherries in a food processor and reduce to a paste. Add the coconut oil and coconut and pulse until combined.

Add the salt, vanilla, cacao powder, nut butter and rice malt syrup and process until the mixture sticks together.

Line a rectangular baking tin, measuring about 34 x 23 cm (13½ x 9 inches) and 5 cm (2 inches) deep, with baking paper. Press the mixture into the tin and freeze for up to 1 hour.

Whisk the chocolate coating ingredients together in a bowl.

Place a sheet of baking paper on the kitchen bench, then set a wire baking rack on top.

Remove the baking tin from the freezer and cut the cherry mixture into bite-sized pieces.

Dip each piece in the chocolate and place on the wire rack to allow the excess chocolate to drain off.

Store in an airtight container in the fridge. The cherry bites will keep for 2–3 weeks.

TIP *You can replace the nut butter with seed butter to make this recipe nut-allergy friendly.*

125 g (4½ oz/1 cup) dried cherries
60 ml (2 fl oz/¼ cup) melted coconut oil
360 g (12¾ oz/4 cups) desiccated
    coconut
⅛ teaspoon Himalayan salt
1 teaspoon vanilla powder
2 tablespoons raw cacao powder
2 tablespoons macadamia or almond
    butter (see tip)
45 ml (1½ fl oz) rice malt syrup

Chocolate coating
375 ml (13 fl oz/1½ cups) melted
    coconut oil
175 g (6 oz/1½ cups) raw cacao powder
185 ml (6 fl oz/¾ cup) maple syrup

Repeatedly on my remake list, these large cookies hit the spot with each bite. The tahini and cacao butter in the cookie contribute to the rich nutty flavour, and the glossy peanut butter swirl is lick-your-lips good.
The only challenge is stopping at one.

Peanut butter swirl chocolate cookies

MAKES 4 ⊗ R + VGN + DF + GF + RSF

200 g (7 oz/3 cups) shredded coconut
150 g (5½ oz/1 cup) medjool dates, pitted
2 tablespoons raw cacao powder
1 teaspoon vanilla powder
2 teaspoons melted cacao butter
2 tablespoons rice malt syrup
2 tablespoons tahini

Chocolate peanut butter swirl
70 g (2½ oz/¼ cup) smooth peanut butter
1 teaspoon coconut oil
75 g (2½ oz/½ cup) chopped sugar-free dark chocolate

Place the coconut, dates, cacao powder and vanilla in a food processor. Blend until broken down into small pieces.

Add the cacao butter, rice malt syrup and tahini. Process until the mixture is well combined and sticky.

Roll the cookie dough out on a kitchen bench or cutting board and cut out four round cookie shapes using an 8 cm (3¼ inch) cookie cutter. Transfer to a tray and place in the freezer to firm up while you make the topping.

Place the peanut butter and coconut oil in a small saucepan over low heat and whisk until well combined. Add the chocolate and leave until it just begins to melt, then stir briefly and remove from the heat.

Swirl a tablespoon of the topping over each cookie and set in the fridge for 2–3 hours.

Store the cookies in an airtight container in the fridge. They will keep for 2–4 weeks.

TIP *If you'd like the cookies to be raw or nut free, omit the chocolate peanut butter swirl.*

I adore this recipe. It's hugely popular, and for good reason. Made without flour, sugar, butter or an oven, these biscuits taste way too good to be a raw, healthy version of those cream-filled store-bought chocolate ones.

If I had to convince you to make just one chocolatey recipe in this book, it would be this one. Heaven in a bite.

Raw Rios

MAKES 4 LARGE COOKIES ✕ R + VGN + DF + GF + RSF

Put the biscuit ingredients in a food processor and blend until the mixture has a dough-like consistency.

Roll the mixture into a large ball and place it on a cutting board. Using a rolling pin, flatten it out to about 5 mm (¼ inch) thick.

Cut out eight circle shapes, using an 8 cm (3¼ inch) cookie cutter. Refrigerate for 2–3 hours, or until firm. (To speed things up, you can freeze the cookie rounds for about 1 hour.)

Clean out the food processor. To make the filling, drain the cashews and place in the processor. Add the remaining filling ingredients and blitz until creamy and smooth.

Spread the filling over half the chilled cookies. Top with the remaining cookie halves and sandwich them together.

The cookies will keep in an airtight container in the fridge for 7 days, or in the freezer for 6–8 weeks.

Biscuits

75 g (2½ oz/¾ cup) pecans

150 g (5½ oz/1 cup) medjool dates, pitted

pinch of Himalayan salt

1 teaspoon vanilla powder

25 g (1 oz/¼ cup) raw cacao powder

Filling

150 g (5½ oz/1 cup) cashews, soaked for at least 2 hours

1 tablespoon coconut oil

1 tablespoon rice malt syrup

1 teaspoon vanilla powder

These chewy raw chocolate and oat cookies are really easy to make, and just as easy to eat. Quinoa flakes are a fabulous source of plant-based protein and dietary fibre, and add a complex flavour to the nutty taste. These cookies are always a hit with children and a great alternative to store-bought biscuits.

Chewy oat cookies with chocolate

MAKES 6 ⊗ R + VGN + DF + GF + RSF

90 g (3¼ oz/1 cup) gluten-free rolled (porridge) oats, plus extra for sprinkling

100 g (3½ oz/1 cup) quinoa flakes

90 g (3¼ oz/1 cup) desiccated coconut

1 teaspoon vanilla powder

⅛ teaspoon Himalayan salt

185 ml (6 fl oz/¾ cup) rice malt syrup

3 tablespoons nut or seed butter

1 tablespoon tahini

Chocolate maple drizzle

80 ml (2½ fl oz/⅓ cup) melted coconut oil

55 g (2 oz/½ cup) raw cacao powder

45 ml (1½ fl oz) maple syrup

Place the oats, quinoa flakes, coconut, vanilla and salt in a food processor and reduce to small crumbs. Add the rice malt syrup, nut butter and tahini. Pulse until the mixture is well combined and sticky.

Roll the mixture onto a clean kitchen bench or cutting board. Cut into six rounds using an 8 cm (3¼ inch) cookie cutter. Place on a tray and freeze for 1–2 hours, or until firm.

In a bowl, whisk the chocolate maple drizzle ingredients together.

Place a tablespoon of the chocolate drizzle mixture in the middle of each cookie and sprinkle with some extra oats.

Keep the cookies in the freezer and remove 30 minutes before serving. They will keep in the freezer, in an airtight container, for up to 8 weeks.

TIP *To make this recipe nut free, replace the nut butter with a seed butter, such as sunflower or pepita (pumpkin seed), or extra tahini.*

A flourless, super healthy and deliciously fudgy brownie that will leave a lasting impression.

I wasn't initially convinced black beans would work well in desserts, and experimented multiple times before finally landing this recipe. Nowadays I preach about this black bean and chocolate combo, as I just love these brownies so much. I hope I can assure the cynic in you to give these a try. You won't regret it.

Black bean brownies

MAKES 6 ✖ **VGN + DF + GF + RSF + NF**

3 ripe bananas
260 g (9¼ oz/1½ cups) cooked or tinned black beans, rinsed and drained
25 g (1 oz/¼ cup) quinoa flakes
85 g (3 oz/¾ cup) raw cacao powder
1 teaspoon vanilla powder
⅛ teaspoon Himalayan salt
1½ teaspoons gluten-free baking powder
60 ml (2 fl oz/¼ cup) melted coconut oil
170 ml (5½ fl oz/⅔ cup) rice malt syrup

Preheat the oven to 160°C (315°F). Line a baking tin, measuring about 21.5 x 11.5 cm (8 x 4 inches), and about 7 cm (2¾ inches) deep, with baking paper.

Place the bananas in a food processor and blend until smooth. Add all the other ingredients and blend again until smooth.

Pour the batter into the baking tin, then bake for 30–35 minutes, or until the brownie is dense, yet still moist in the centre when tested with a skewer.

Remove from the oven and leave to cool in the tin, then cut into slices to serve.

Store in an airtight container in the fridge, or at room temperature. Best enjoyed within 2–3 days.

TIP *If you prefer a less moist result, you can bake the brownies at a lower temperature for a little longer.*

Nougat, caramel and chocolate: a winning combination. Throw in some dates and coconut oil and you're on an even bigger winner. If you are trying to convince someone to embrace healthy raw treats, or to at least try one, this is the recipe for you.

You'll need to plan ahead for these addictive bars as there is some soaking required, as well as freezing time between each layer.

Galaxy bars

MAKES 5 ❌ R + VGN + DF + GF + RSF

Start by making the nougat base. Drain the almonds and cashews and dry them with paper towel. Place in a food processor with the rice malt syrup and lucuma powder and process until well combined. Add 1–2 tablespoons water if your mixture seems too thick and doesn't blend well.

Line a slab tin, about 19.5 cm (7½ inches) square and 4 cm (1½ inches) deep, with baking paper. Spread the nougat mixture in the bottom of the tin. Freeze for 1–2 hours while making the caramel.

Clean out the food processor. Place the caramel ingredients in the processor, add 2 tablespoons water and blend until smooth and creamy.

Spread the caramel over the nougat base and freeze for at least 2 hours.

Whisk the chocolate coating ingredients together in a bowl.

Remove the tin from the freezer and cut the mixture into five rectangular pieces.

Place a sheet of baking paper on the kitchen bench, then set a wire baking rack on top.

Spear the bars with a fork and dip them into the chocolate mixture, then place on the wire rack to allow the excess chocolate to drain off.

Once the chocolate has set, store the bars in an airtight container in the fridge, where they will keep for up to 1 week, or in the freezer for up to 4–6 weeks.

Nougat base
80 g (2¾ oz/½ cup) almonds, soaked for 4 hours
75 g (2½ oz/½ cup) cashews, soaked for 4 hours
2 tablespoons rice malt syrup
1 tablespoon lucuma powder

Caramel
8 medjool dates, pitted
1 tablespoon almond butter
1 tablespoon melted coconut oil
2 tablespoons rice malt syrup
⅛ teaspoon Himalayan salt
½ teaspoon vanilla powder

Chocolate coating
125 ml (4 fl oz/½ cup) melted coconut oil
40 g (1½ oz/⅓ cup) raw cacao powder
60 ml (2 fl oz/¼ cup) maple syrup
½ teaspoon vanilla powder

Creamy, delicious chunks of gold, these caramel slice bars are the real deal, featuring a crumbly nutty biscuit base, smooth caramel centre and silky chocolate top. They're also free of dairy, gluten and sugar, so you can enjoy them guilt free.

Caramel slice

MAKES 8 ✖ R + VGN + DF + GF + RSF

To make the cashew base, put the cashews in a food processor and chop into small pieces. Add the coconut and pulse briefly. Add the dates and rice malt syrup, then process until combined and sticky.

Line a slab tin, measuring about 34 x 23 cm (13½ x 9 inches) and 5 cm (2 inches) deep, with baking paper. Evenly press the cashew mixture into the tin, then place in the freezer while making the caramel.

Clean out the food processor, then add all the caramel ingredients and process until smooth.

Spread the caramel over the cashew base. Freeze for 2–3 hours, or until firm.

For the chocolate layer, put all the ingredients in a bowl and beat with a hand whisk until well incorporated.

Spread the chocolate evenly over the caramel layer and freeze for 1–2 hours, or until firm.

Remove from the freezer about 30 minutes before serving.

Cut into slices to serve.

The slice will keep in the freezer for up to 8 weeks, sliced and stored in an airtight container.

Cashew base

225 g (8 oz/1½ cups) cashews

45 g (1½ oz/½ cup) desiccated coconut

8–10 medjool dates, pitted

3 tablespoons rice malt syrup

Caramel

150 g (5½ oz/1 cup) medjool dates, pitted

60 ml (2 fl oz/¼ cup) melted coconut oil

125 ml (4 fl oz/½ cup) tahini or almond butter

125 ml (4 fl oz/½ cup) rice malt syrup

1 teaspoon vanilla powder

pinch of Himalayan salt

Chocolate layer

40 g (1½ oz/⅓ cup) raw cacao powder

125 ml (4 fl oz/½ cup) melted coconut oil

60 ml (2 fl oz/¼ cup) maple syrup

½ teaspoon carob powder (optional)

Chewy spiced donuts with chocolate glaze: you are pure bliss! These raw beauties are really quick to whip up and hit the spot each time. They're also high in dietary fibre due to the inclusion of oats, psyllium husks and chia seeds, so you can enjoy these treats knowing you are doing good for your body. They are a super-cute addition to your party table, and an absolute knockout for your tastebuds.

Raw donuts

MAKES 12 ⊗ R + VGN + DF + GF + RSF

Place the oats in a food processor and blitz to the consistency of fine crumbs. Add the shredded coconut and process until just combined.

Add the chia seeds, psyllium husks, vanilla, cinnamon and salt and process until just combined.

Add the nut butter, dates and rice malt syrup and process until well incorporated and sticky.

Press the mixture into two oiled six-hole donut tins and place in the freezer for 2–3 hours. If you don't have a donut tin, roll the mixture into ball shapes, about 6 cm (2 inches) in diameter. Make a hole in the centre of each ball, then flatten slightly. Place on a plate lined with baking paper and set in the freezer.

Once the donuts have set, make the glaze. Add the dark chocolate to a small heatproof bowl and place over a saucepan of simmering water. Stir until melted, then remove from the heat.

Melt the caramel chocolate in another small heatproof bowl set over a saucepan of simmering water, to make a caramel glaze.

Remove the donuts from their tin. Place on a wire baking rack, set over a sheet of baking paper to catch the drips. Drizzle your chocolate glaze and caramel glaze over the donuts, creating a two-tone effect. (If you want to be really fancy, you could also sprinkle the glazed donuts with cacao nibs or shredded coconut!)

The donuts can be stored in an airtight container in the fridge for up to 1 week, or in the freezer for 4–6 weeks.

TIP *To make this recipe nut free, use tahini instead of nut butter. If you can't find a vegan sugar-free caramel chocolate, double the quantity of the dark chocolate to replace the caramel in the glaze.*

180 g (6 oz/2 cups) gluten-free rolled (porridge) oats
65 g (2 oz/1 cup) shredded coconut
40 g (1 oz/¼ cup) chia seeds
1 tablespoon psyllium husks
1 teaspoon vanilla powder
2 teaspoons ground cinnamon
⅛ teaspoon Himalayan salt
2 tablespoons nut or seed butter, such as peanut, cashew or tahini (see tip)
8–10 medjool dates, pitted
125 ml (4 fl oz/½ cup) rice malt syrup

Two-toned choc caramel glaze
150 g (5 oz/1 cup) chopped dark sugar-free chocolate
150 g (5 oz/1 cup) chopped caramel sugar-free chocolate (see tip)

I'm often amazed that we can use basic natural ingredients to make such delicious treats. These caramel, chocolate and shortbread bars are the perfect example.

They are great straight out of the freezer, any time of the day. Whenever I make a batch, they're eaten up in a heartbeat. I challenge you to stop at just one.

Caramel stix bar

MAKES 5 ✖ R + VGN + DF + GF + RSF

To make the shortbread, place the macadamias in a food processor and blend into small crumbs. Add the vanilla, salt and 45 ml (1½ fl oz) of the rice malt syrup. Blend until just combined, adding the remaining rice malt syrup if needed to bring the mixture together.

Line a small slab tin, about 19.5 cm (7½ inches) square and 4 cm (1½ inches) deep, with baking paper. Press the shortbread evenly into the tin and freeze while you make the caramel.

Clean out the food processor. Add the caramel ingredients and 1 tablespoon water and blend until smooth and creamy.

Spread the caramel over the shortbread and freeze for at least 1 hour.

In a bowl, whisk the chocolate ingredients together until well incorporated.

Remove the tin from the freezer and cut the slice into long rectangular bars.

Place a sheet of baking paper on the kitchen bench, then set a wire baking rack on top. Dip the bars into the chocolate, coating them all over, and place on the wire rack to allow the excess to drain off.

The bars will keep in an airtight container in the freezer for 6–8 weeks. They are best eaten within 5–10 minutes of being removed from the freezer.

Shortbread

155 g (5½ oz/1 cup) macadamia nuts
½ teaspoon vanilla powder
⅛ teaspoon Himalayan salt
45–60 ml (1½–2 fl oz) rice malt syrup

Caramel

10–12 medjool dates, pitted
3 tablespoons almond butter
⅛ teaspoon Himalayan salt

Chocolate

40 g (1½ oz/⅓ cup) raw cacao powder
125 ml (4 fl oz/½ cup) melted coconut oil
60 ml (2 fl oz/¼ cup) maple syrup
½ teaspoon vanilla powder

I love these raw cookies for so many reasons. The flavour is mildly nutty, the texture perfectly chewy, and the recipe very adaptable. Each one is full of nutrition, boasting high levels of calcium, protein and healthy fats. They are perfect for both adults and children, and easily added to lunch boxes. They are incredibly easy to make, and best of all, delicious! If you find the taste of tahini a bit overpowering, use almond or cashew butter instead.

Raw coconut tahini cookies

MAKES 12 ⊗ R + VGN + DF + GF + RSF

In a mixing bowl, combine the coconut, vanilla powder, mesquite powder and salt.

Add the tahini, rice malt syrup and coconut oil and mix well.

Freeze for 5–10 minutes, or until the mixture is firm.

Roll the chilled mixture out on a cutting board or kitchen bench, between 5 mm (¼ inch) and 1 cm (½ inch) thick.

Using an 8 cm (3¼ inch) cookie cutter, cut out 12 cookie rounds.

Place an almond in the middle of each cookie and freeze for at least 30 minutes to set.

Once set, store the cookies in an airtight container in the fridge. They will keep in the fridge for 5 days, or in the freezer for 8 weeks.

TIP *To make this recipe nut free, omit the almonds, or replace them with pepitas (pumpkin seeds) or sunflower seeds.*

225 g (8 oz/2½ cups) desiccated coconut

1 teaspoon vanilla powder

1 tablespoon mesquite powder

⅛ teaspoon Himalayan salt

135 g (4¾ oz/½ cup) tahini

125 ml (4 fl oz/½ cup) plus 2 tablespoons rice malt syrup

125 ml (4 fl oz/½ cup) melted coconut oil

12 almonds (see tip)

*A classic dessert given a healthier spin. With its
layers of chocolatey coffee, biscuit and cream, you
will find it hard to believe this raw, vegan wholefood
version isn't the real thing.*
  Pure decadence in a cup, and totally guilt free.

Tiramisu

SERVES 2 ✖ R + VGN + DF + GF + RSF

To make the base, put the almonds, pecans and cashews in a food processor and blend until small pieces form. Add the dates and salt and process until well blended and sticky.

Press evenly into two 500 ml (17 fl oz/2 cup) glasses and freeze while making the coffee layer.

Clean out the food processor. To make the coffee filling, drain the cashews and blitz in the processor with the almonds, rice malt syrup and coconut milk until well combined.

Add the coffee and coconut oil and pulse until well combined. Add the cacao powder and salt and blend until you achieve a smooth consistency.

Pour the coffee layer over the base. Top each glass with three biscuit halves and refrigerate while you prepare the cream layer.

Clean out the processor again.

Drain the cashews and place in the processor. Add the coconut milk, rice malt syrup and coconut oil and blend until the mixture is smooth and the nuts have a creamy consistency. Add the lemon juice, vanilla powder and salt and pulse until smooth.

Spread the cream over the biscuits, then garnish with shaved chocolate. Refrigerate for at least 1–2 hours before serving.

The tiramisu will keep in the fridge for 2–3 days.

TIP In the coffee layer, instead of espresso coffee you could use 3 teaspoons instant coffee mixed with 2 tablespoons hot water. If you'd like the recipe to be fully raw, omit the store-bought biscuits in the coffee layer. (The unfilled Jam biscuit sandwiches on page 160 would work well, but your dessert won't be fully raw.)

Base
80 g (2¾ oz/½ cup) almonds, soaked for 8 hours
35 g (1¼ oz/⅓ cup) pecans
50 g (1¾ oz/⅓ cup) cashews
5 medjool dates, pitted
⅛ teaspoon Himalayan salt

Coffee layer
75 g (2½ oz/½ cup) cashews, soaked for 8 hours
80 g (2¾ oz/½ cup) almonds, soaked for 8 hours
2 tablespoons rice malt syrup
60 ml (2 fl oz/¼ cup) coconut milk
60 ml (2 fl oz/¼ cup) espresso coffee
1 teaspoon coconut oil
2 teaspoons raw cacao powder
⅛ teaspoon Himalayan salt
3 store-bought vegan gluten-free biscuits (see tip), cut in half

Cream layer
150 g (5½ oz/1 cup) cashews, soaked for 4 hours
170 ml (5½ fl oz/⅔ cup) coconut milk
2 tablespoons rice malt syrup
1 teaspoon coconut oil
¼ teaspoon lemon juice
1 teaspoon vanilla powder
⅛ teaspoon Himalayan salt
2 tablespoons shaved sugar-free dark chocolate

Chocolate and hazelnut: who can resist? These easy no-bake brownies are almost too good to be true. You don't need a whole lot of time or ingredients to get these ones happening — but you may find it hard to resist the whole slab!

Raw hazelnut brownies

MAKES 14 ⊗ R + VGN + DF + GF + RSF

270 g (9½ oz/2 cups) hazelnuts
265 g (9½ oz/2½ cups) shredded coconut
85 g (3 oz/¾ cup) raw cacao powder
650 g (1 lb 7 oz/4 cups) almonds
⅛ teaspoon Himalayan salt
225 g (8 oz/1½ cups) medjool dates
250 ml (9 fl oz/1 cup) rice malt syrup

Ganache
450 g (1 lb/3 cups) chopped sugar-free dark chocolate
500 ml (17 fl oz/2 cups) coconut milk

Place the hazelnuts, coconut, cacao powder, almonds and salt in a food processor and process into small crumbs.

Add the dates and rice malt syrup and process until the mixture is well combined and sticky.

Line a 24 cm (9½ inch) square cake tin, about 5 cm (2 inches) deep, with baking paper. Transfer half the brownie mixture to the tin and press down evenly. Set the remaining brownie mixture aside.

To make the chocolate ganache, add the chocolate and coconut milk to a saucepan and stir over medium heat until the chocolate has melted and thickened. Remove from the heat. Using a tablespoon, randomly dollop about 6 tablespoons of the ganache over the brownie base. Freeze for 10–20 minutes.

Remove the tin from the freezer and press the remaining brownie mixture evenly over the top. Pour the rest of the ganache over the brownie, spreading it evenly.

Freeze for 3–4 hours, or until set.

Remove from the freezer 30–40 minutes before serving. Cut into slices to serve. The brownies will keep in an airtight container in the freezer for 4–6 weeks.

One of the great things about raw treats is that a little goes a long way. The pure raw ingredients in this bar make each portion rich and fulfilling, so you don't need a lot to satisfy. They also give a superior flavour — you won't believe how good this chocolate and caramel bar tastes!

Peanut snack bars

MAKES 9 ✕ R + VGN + DF + GF + RSF

Start by preparing the base. Put the oats, cashews, almonds, coconut and salt in a food processor and blend until the ingredients have broken down into small pieces. Add the rice malt syrup and coconut paste and process until mixture is well combined and sticky.

Line a 24 cm (9½ inch) square cake or slab tin, about 5 cm (2 inches) deep, with baking paper. Press the mixture into the tin and freeze while making the caramel layer.

Clean out the food processor. To make the caramel, put the dates, peanut butter, vanilla, coconut oil and salt in the processor. Blend until smooth, adding 1 tablespoon water (or a little more if needed) to bring the mixture together.

Spread the caramel over the base. Scatter the peanuts over the top, pressing them in lightly, then freeze for 1 hour.

In a bowl, whisk the chocolate drizzle ingredients together until well incorporated. Drizzle the mixture over the caramel and peanuts and freeze for at least 2–4 hours, until completely firm.

Remove from the freezer 20–30 minutes before serving. Cut into rectangular bars to serve.

The bars will keep in an airtight container in the freezer for 6–8 weeks.

Base

90 g (3¼ oz/1 cup) gluten-free rolled (porridge) oats

150 g (5½ oz/1 cup) cashews

160 g (5½ oz/1 cup) almonds

90 g (3¼ oz/1 cup) desiccated coconut

pinch of Himalayan salt

125 ml (4 fl oz/½ cup) rice malt syrup

2 tablespoons coconut butter, mixed with 1 tablespoon boiling water

Caramel

300 g (10½ oz/2 cups) medjool dates, pitted and soaked in boiling water for 1–2 hours

2 tablespoons smooth peanut butter

1 teaspoon vanilla powder

1 tablespoon coconut oil

pinch of Himalayan salt

70 g (1½ oz/½ cup) peanuts

Chocolate drizzle

125 ml (4 fl oz/½ cup) melted coconut oil

85 g (3 oz/¾ cup) raw cacao powder

60 ml (2 fl oz/¼ cup) maple syrup

A classic peppermint slice — only this one is full of wholesome ingredients. As well as being a beautiful addition to sweet treats, peppermint is a powerful natural healing agent and has long been used to aid digestion and treat nausea. It pairs beautifully with chocolate, while the buckwheat groats in the base give this slice the perfect crunch factor.

This slice is great as a treat, and is especially suitable for parties and entertaining.

Peppermint slice

MAKES 8 ⊗ R + VGN + DF + GF + RSF

Base

100 g (3½ oz/1 cup) pecans

90 g (3¼ oz/½ cup) activated buckwheat groats

55 g (2 oz/½ cup) raw cacao powder

1 teaspoon vanilla powder

6 medjool dates, pitted

60 ml (2 fl oz/¼ cup) rice malt syrup

Peppermint filling

300 g (10½ oz/2 cups) cashews, soaked for 15–30 minutes

125 ml (4 fl oz/½ cup) melted cacao butter (see tip)

125 ml (4 fl oz/½ cup) rice malt syrup

1 teaspoon natural peppermint extract

Chocolate ganache

115 g (4 oz/¾ cup) cashews, soaked for 1–2 hours

125 ml (4 fl oz/½ cup) melted coconut oil

60 ml (2 fl oz/¼ cup) rice malt syrup

55 g (2 oz/½ cup) raw cacao powder

½ teaspoon vanilla powder

To make the base, put the pecans in a food processor and blend into small pieces. Add the buckwheat groats, cacao powder and vanilla and pulse until well combined. Add the dates and rice malt syrup and process until the mixture is well combined and sticky.

Line a loaf (bar) tin, measuring about 24 x 13 cm (9 x 5 inches), and about 6 cm (2 inches) deep, with baking paper. Press the mixture into the tin and refrigerate while making the peppermint filling.

Clean out the processor. Drain the cashews and place in the processor with the cacao butter, rice malt syrup and 125 ml (4 fl oz/½ cup) water. Blend until the nuts have reached a smooth consistency — you want the filling to be smooth.

Fold the peppermint extract through, then pour the mixture over the base. Freeze for at least 2–3 hours, until firm.

Clean out the processor again. To make the chocolate ganache, drain the cashews and process with the coconut oil and rice malt syrup until smooth. Add the cacao powder and vanilla and pulse until well combined.

Spread the ganache over the firm filling, then return to the freezer for up to 6 hours, or until set.

Remove from the freezer about 30 minutes before serving. Cut into slices to serve.

The peppermint slice will keep in an airtight container in the freezer for 6–8 weeks.

TIP *Cacao butter is rock solid! For this recipe, in which it replaces softened butter, it needs to be in liquid form. To turn it into a liquid, simply place some cacao butter in a heatproof bowl over a saucepan of simmering water. Stir the cacao butter with a whisk or a spatula, checking with a thermometer to ensure the temperature does not rise above 48°C (118°F), in order to keep all the valuable nutrients intact. If it starts rising above this temperature, remove the bowl from the heat; the cacao butter should now be warm enough to finish melting on its own.*

THE PARTY SPREAD

Nourish your kids

Baked cinnamon
donuts *194*

×

Raw ombre
birthday cake *198*

Rocky road *194*

×

Chocolate cupcakes *195*

I am officially obsessed with these sweet mini donuts. A breeze to make, they are also a hit with my kids. I've used a mixture of buckwheat and teff flour to create the sponge-like dough that we love about donuts. Teff flour is gluten free, versatile and adds a lovely nutty flavour to baked goods. You should be able to find it in your local health food store, and definitely online.

Rocky road is a chocoholic's dream, and I adore this version — not only is it deliciously indulgent, it takes just minutes to whip up. I love the combination of nuts and fruit and how they sink right into the lush melted chocolate...

This recipe is pretty flexible, so you can easily swap the nuts and dried fruit for your own favourites — just be sure to use the same measurements.

Baked cinnamon donuts

MAKES 12 ✪ VGN + DF + GF + RSF + NF

130 g (4½ oz/1 cup) buckwheat flour

70 g (2½ oz/½ cup) teff flour

1 tablespoon potato flour

1 tablespoon coconut flour

2 teaspoons gluten-free baking powder

⅛ teaspoon Himalayan salt

500 ml (17 fl oz/2 cups) coconut milk or other non-dairy milk

2 tablespoons rice malt syrup

1 tablespoon melted coconut oil, plus an extra 2 tablespoons for brushing

1 tablespoon ground cinnamon

100 g (3½ oz/½ cup) granulated coconut sugar

Preheat the oven to 170°C (325°F).

In a large bowl, combine the buckwheat flour, teff flour, potato flour, coconut flour, baking powder and salt.

Add the coconut milk, rice malt syrup and 1 tablespoon coconut oil and whisk well.

Spoon the mixture into two lightly oiled six-hole donut tins. Do not overfill the donut holes, as your donuts will need a little room to expand.

Transfer to the oven and bake for 10–12 minutes, or until just cooked and lightly browned. For springy donuts, make sure you don't bake them too long: just cooked and very lightly browned is what you're aiming for.

Remove the donuts from the tins, then lightly brush on both sides with more coconut oil.

Combine the cinnamon and coconut sugar, generously sprinkle all over the donuts and serve immediately. They are best enjoyed warm, straight out of the oven.

Rocky road

MAKES 8 ✪ R + VGN + DF + GF + RSF

60 g (2¼ oz/½ cup) macadamia nuts

30 g (1 oz/¼ cup) unsweetened dried cranberries

20 g (¾ oz/¾ cup) puffed rice, or 30 g (1 oz/¾ cup) puffed quinoa

20 g (¾ oz/¼ cup) shredded coconut

30 g (1 oz/¼ cup) cacao nibs

500 g (1 lb 2 oz) dark unsweetened chocolate, chopped

Line a loaf (bar) tin, measuring about 24 x 13 cm (9½ x 5 inches), and about 6 cm (2½ inches) deep, with baking paper.

Combine the macadamias, cranberries, puffed rice or quinoa, coconut and cacao nibs in a bowl.

Place the dark chocolate in a small heatproof bowl and set over a saucepan of simmering water, ensuring the base of the bowl doesn't touch the water. Stir the chocolate until it has melted, then remove from the heat.

Pour the melted chocolate over the dry ingredients and stir to combine. Pour the mixture into the loaf tin and set in the fridge overnight.

When you are ready to serve, remove from the tin and cut into bite-sized pieces using a sharp knife.

Store in an airtight container in the fridge; the rocky road will keep for up to 2 weeks.

It wouldn't be a party without cupcakes. These ones are free of gluten, refined sugar, dairy, eggs, artificial colourings and nuts. Hard to believe, right?

These cupcakes are made with a variety of gluten-free flours, but your party guests won't even know they're free of all the usual suspects.

I hope you and your family enjoy these beauties as much as we do.

Chocolate cupcakes

MAKES 18 ✖ VGN + DF + GF + RSF

Start by making the frosting. Boil, steam or bake the sweet potato until tender. Leave to cool, then place in a food processor with the remaining frosting ingredients and blend until smooth and creamy. Scrape the frosting into a clean bowl, then cover and refrigerate for 2–3 hours, to let it cool and firm up.

Preheat the oven to 170°C (325°F). Line 18 holes of two muffin tins (80 ml/2½ fl oz/⅓ cup capacity) with paper cases.

Sift the rice flour, potato flour, sorghum flour, tapioca flour and cacao powder into a large bowl. Stir in the coconut sugar, xanthan gum, baking powder, bicarbonate of soda and salt.

In a separate bowl, mix together the coconut milk, grapeseed oil, apple sauce, water, vinegar and vanilla. Add to the flour mixture and fold through until well combined.

Scoop the mixture into the paper cases, then bake for 20–25 minutes, or until a skewer inserted into the middle of the cupcakes comes out clean.

Remove from the oven and leave to cool completely.

Using a piping (icing) bag, pipe the frosting over the cooled cupcakes.

Being gluten free, these cupcakes are best enjoyed the same day they are made.

TIP *To make the frosting nut free, use sunflower or pepita (pumpkin seed) butter instead of the cashew butter.*

125 g (4½ oz/¾ cup) white rice flour

90 g (3¼ oz/½ cup) potato flour

65 g (2¼ oz/½ cup) sorghum flour

30 g (1 oz/¼ cup) tapioca flour

55 g (2 oz/½ cup) raw cacao powder

200 g (7 oz/1 cup) granulated coconut sugar

1 teaspoon xanthan gum

1 teaspoon gluten-free baking powder

1 teaspoon bicarbonate of soda (baking soda)

¼ teaspoon Himalayan salt

185 ml (6 fl oz/¾ cup) coconut milk

80 ml (2½ fl oz/⅓ cup) grapeseed oil

60 ml (2 fl oz/¼ cup) apple sauce

310 ml (10¾ fl oz/1¼ cups) warm water

1 teaspoon white vinegar or apple cider vinegar

1 teaspoon natural vanilla extract

Frosting

2 orange sweet potatoes, chopped

75 g (2½ oz/½ cup) medjool dates, pitted

125 ml (4 fl oz/½ cup) coconut milk

1 tablespoon cashew butter

1 teaspoon ground cinnamon

3 tablespoons raw cacao powder

YOUR HEALTH IS
A PRIORITY, NOT
AN AFTERTHOUGHT

What's a birthday without a birthday cake? This one is a knockout. The flavours, the colours, the textures... there's a whole bunch of reasons why this cake should be on your next birthday hit list. Can't wait for you to try it!

Organic blueberry and strawberry powder gives a vibrant, punchy taste to the cashew cream, and the most unbelievable colour. I recommend sourcing them online or from a health food store to get the best results for this super special cheesecake.

Raw ombre birthday cake

SERVES 20 ✪ R + VGN + DF + GF + RSF

Base

175 g (6 oz/1½ cups) walnuts

100 g (3½ oz/1½ cups) shredded coconut

120 g (4 oz/1 cup) dried cranberries (preferably sugar free, sweetened with apple juice)

60 ml (2 fl oz/¼ cup) rice malt syrup

⅛ teaspoon Himalayan salt

Vanilla layer

625 g (1 lb 6 oz/4 cups) cashews, soaked for 4 hours

250 ml (9 fl oz/1 cup) melted coconut oil

310 ml (10¾ fl oz/1¼ cups) rice malt syrup

250 ml (9 fl oz/1 cup) coconut milk or other non-dairy milk

170–250 ml (5½–9 fl oz/⅔–1 cup) filtered water (or non-dairy milk)

1 tablespoon lemon juice

1 teaspoon vanilla powder

⅛ teaspoon Himalayan salt

First blueberry layer

625 g (1 lb 6 oz/4 cups) cashews, soaked for 4 hours

250 ml (9 fl oz/1 cup) melted coconut oil

310 ml (10¾ fl oz/1¼ cups) rice malt syrup

250 ml (9 fl oz/1 cup) coconut milk or other non-dairy milk

170–250 ml (5½–9 fl oz/⅔–1 cup) filtered water (or non-dairy milk)

1 tablespoon lemon juice

1 tablespoon blueberry powder (or 1–2 cups fresh blueberries, depending on how intense you'd like the colour and flavour)

⅛ teaspoon Himalayan salt

Second blueberry layer

625 g (1 lb 6 oz/4 cups) cashews, soaked for 4 hours

250 ml (9 fl oz/1 cup) melted coconut oil

310 ml (10¾ fl oz/1¼ cups) rice malt syrup

250 ml (9 fl oz/1 cup) coconut milk or other non-dairy milk

170–250 ml (5½–9 fl oz/⅔–1 cup) filtered water (or non-dairy milk)

1 tablespoon lemon juice

2 tablespoons blueberry powder (or 2–3 cups fresh blueberries, depending on how intense you'd like the colour and flavour)

⅛ teaspoon Himalayan salt

Dreamy bliss balls

160 g (5½ oz/1 cup) almonds

115 g (4 oz/1 cup) walnuts

130 g (4½ oz/2 cups) shredded coconut

90 g (3¼ oz/½ cup) activated buckwheat groats

60 g (2¼ oz/½ cup) dried cranberries (preferably sugar free, sweetened with apple juice)

4 medjool dates, pitted

2–3 tablespoons rice malt syrup

2 tablespoons strawberry powder, or 4–5 dried or freeze-dried strawberries

½ teaspoon grated lemon zest

90 g (3¼ oz/1 cup) desiccated coconut

1–2 tablespoons blueberry powder (or extra desiccated coconut)

To decorate

1 lemon, sliced

2–3 tablespoons desiccated coconut

a small handful of organic edible flowers (optional)

To make the base

Place the walnuts and coconut in a food processor and chop into small pieces. Add the remaining ingredients and process until well combined and sticky.

Line a 24 cm (9½ inch) square cake tin, about 5 cm (2 inches) deep, with baking paper. Press the mixture into the tin and freeze while making the vanilla and blueberry layers.

To prepare the layers

Clean out the food processor. To prepare the vanilla layer, drain and rinse the cashews and place in the processor with the remaining vanilla layer ingredients. Blitz until the mixture is smooth and creamy. Pour into a bowl and place in the freezer while making the other layers.

To make the first blueberry layer, rinse out the processor. Drain and rinse the cashews and add to the processor with the remaining ingredients. Blitz until smooth and creamy, then pour into another bowl and freeze for 1 hour.

Rinse out the processor and make the second blueberry layer in the same way. Pour into a third bowl and set in the freezer for 1 hour.

Reserve about ½ cup of the vanilla layer mixture to decorate the cake, keeping it covered in the fridge. Spread the rest of the vanilla mixture evenly over the cake base and freeze for at least 1 hour.

Spread the first blueberry layer over the vanilla and freeze for at least another hour.

Repeat with the second blueberry layer and set in the freezer overnight.

For the dreamy bliss balls

Clean out the food processor. Add the almonds, walnuts and shredded coconut and blitz until broken down into crumbs. Add the buckwheat groats, cranberries, dates, rice malt syrup, strawberry powder and lemon zest, and process until well combined.

Transfer the mixture to a bowl and refrigerate for 10–15 minutes, to make rolling easier.

Once the mixture has hardened slightly, roll it into balls of varying sizes. Combine the desiccated coconut and blueberry powder and use it to dust the bliss balls.

Freeze the balls for 1–2 hours, or until firm.

To decorate and serve

When ready to serve, remove the cake from the tin and invert onto a serving plate or platter. Place the dreamy bliss balls over the cake.

Using a piping (icing) bag fitted with a star nozzle, pipe the reserved vanilla layer mixture around the cake and bliss balls, wherever you see fit.

Wedge lemon slices between the bliss balls and sprinkle with the desiccated coconut. Garnish with edible flowers, if using.

This cake is best eaten within 30–45 minutes of removing from the freezer. It will keep in an airtight container in the freezer for 6–8 weeks.

These raw swirl cheesecakes are pure heaven. The flavoured swirl delights the eye and complements the light, creamy filling and chocolate base perfectly. Best of all, they contain nothing naughty — only the most nourishing ingredients. Love!

Vanilla swirl cheesecakes

MAKES 6 ✪ R + VGN + DF + GF + RSF

To make the base, put the walnuts and almonds in a food processor and blend into small pieces. Add the coconut, cacao powder and salt and pulse until combined. Add the rice malt syrup and dates and process until the mixture is well combined and sticky.

Press the mixture into six 125 ml (4 fl oz/½ cup) silicone cupcake moulds and refrigerate while making the vanilla filling. (You may have more than enough base mixture for six cakes; store the remainder in the fridge to use next time.)

Clean out the processor. Drain the cashews and place in the processor with the coconut oil, coconut milk, rice malt syrup and 2 tablespoons water. Blend until the nuts have reached a smooth consistency, adding a little more water if needed.

Fold the vanilla through, then pour about three-quarters of the mixture over the bases, reserving some for the swirled toppings. Set in the freezer for at least 3–4 hours.

Place half the remaining filling in a blender. Add the chocolate swirl ingredients and whiz until smooth, then scrape into an airtight container. Clean out the blender, then whiz the remaining filling with the blueberry swirl ingredients until smooth. Scrape into another airtight container. Freeze the swirls for 2–3 hours, or until firm enough to pipe into swirls.

Pop the cakes out of their moulds, onto a serving plate.

Place the chocolate swirl mixture in a piping (icing) bag fitted with a star-shaped nozzle. Starting at the outside edge of a cake, apply pressure to the top of the bag, then pipe in a steady movement around the edge of the cake, building up into a swirl. When you reach the end of the swirl press down slightly, release the pressure and pull up quickly. Pipe the chocolate over two more cakes, then clean out the piping bag and swirl the blueberry mixture over the remaining three cakes.

These cakes are best kept in the freezer, where they will keep in an airtight container for up to 8 weeks.

TIP *I suggest using silicone moulds for these cakes — they will pop out with no effort! A star-shaped piping nozzle works best for these swirls. The size of the star is your choice.*

Base
115 g (4 oz/1 cup) walnuts
80 g (2¾ oz/½ cup) almonds
40 g (1½ oz/½ cup) desiccated coconut
1 tablespoon raw cacao powder
⅛ teaspoon Himalayan salt
60 ml (2 fl oz/¼ cup) rice malt syrup
4–5 medjool dates, pitted

Vanilla filling
600 g (1 lb 5 oz/4 cups) cashews, soaked for at least 4 hours
250 ml (9 fl oz/1 cup) melted coconut oil
500 ml (17 fl oz/2 cups) coconut or almond milk
375 ml (13 fl oz/1½ cups) rice malt syrup
1 teaspoon vanilla powder

Chocolate swirl
1–2 tablespoons raw cacao powder
1 tablespoon cashew butter

Blueberry swirl
1–2 tablespoons blueberry powder
1 tablespoon cashew butter

A fun recipe requiring very little planning, these cookie dough pops are deliciously versatile. I have made them for my children's parties, and they're always a hit.

I personally love to have one after lunch when I need a sweet pick-me-up. The nuts provide the protein to keep me full between meals, while the dates provide a fibre and energy boost. Make a batch and keep them in the fridge.

Cookie dough pops

MAKES 8 ✕ R + VGN + DF + GF + RSF

160 g (5½ oz/1 cup) almonds
150 g (5½ oz/1 cup) cashews
¼ teaspoon vanilla powder
⅛ teaspoon Himalayan salt
225 g (8 oz/1½ cups) medjool dates, pitted

Chocolate coating
125 ml (4 fl oz/½ cup) melted coconut oil
85 g (3 oz/¾ cup) raw cacao powder
60 ml (2 fl oz/¼ cup) maple syrup

Put the almonds and cashews in a food processor and blend into small pieces. Add the vanilla and salt and pulse until well combined. Add the dates and process well, until you have a sticky dough.

Remove the mixture from the processor and roll into eight balls. Freeze for 1–2 hours, or until firm.

Whisk the chocolate coating ingredients together in a bowl. Remove the cookie dough balls from the freezer and insert a skewer through the middle. Dip the balls into the chocolate coating. If you have any chocolate remaining, you can double coat the cookie balls, once the first coating has set.

Store in an airtight container in the fridge. The dough pops will keep for 2–4 weeks in the fridge, or 4–8 weeks in the freezer.

A favourite in our household and sure to become one of yours, this slice is just irresistible. Made with simple wholefood ingredients, it is creamy and well balanced. We enjoy a piece after dinner in place of a traditional dessert and find we really miss it when we don't have a stash in the freezer. An easy crowd-pleaser.

Cookies & cream slice

MAKES 12 ✖ R + VGN + DF + GF + RSF

Place the walnuts and almonds in a food processor and blend into small pieces. Add the buckwheat groats, coconut, cacao powder and salt and pulse until well combined.

Add the dates and rice malt syrup and whiz into a sticky mixture.

Line a rectangular baking tin or slab tin, measuring about 34 x 23 cm (13½ x 9 inches) and 5 cm (2 inches) deep, with baking paper. Press the mixture into the tin and place in the fridge while you make the cream.

Rinse out the food processor. For the cream, drain the cashews and process with the coconut butter, coconut milk and rice malt syrup. The nuts must be broken down and

the cream should be smooth, so keep blending until you achieve a smooth consistency; for a smoother cream, you can use a blender.

Fold the vanilla through, then pour the cream over the base. Scatter the chocolate chips over the cream and set in the freezer for 3–4 hours.

Cut into slices to serve.

The slice will keep in an airtight container in the freezer for 4–8 weeks.

TIP *To soften coconut butter, place the coconut butter jar (minus the lid) in a bowl of boiling water. Stir with a spoon until the butter softens.*

115 g (4 oz/1 cup) walnuts

160 g (5½ oz/1 cup) almonds

90 g (3¼ oz/½ cup) activated buckwheat groats

45 g (1½ oz/½ cup) desiccated coconut

55 g (2 oz/½ cup) raw cacao powder

⅛ teaspoon Himalayan salt

150 g (5½ oz/1 cup) medjool dates, pitted

125 ml (4 fl oz/½ cup) rice malt syrup

3–4 tablespoons sugar-free chocolate chips

Cream

300 g (10½ oz/2 cups) cashews, soaked for at least 4 hours

100 g (3½ oz/1 cup) coconut butter, softened (see tip)

125 ml (4 fl oz/½ cup) coconut milk

125 ml (4 fl oz/½ cup) rice malt syrup

1–2 teaspoons vanilla powder

It astounds me how you can recreate your favourite desserts using simple wholefoods that just so happen to be nature's superfoods. This chocolate mousse is a combination of heart-healthy avocado, cacao and dates, blended with mesquite powder, vanilla, rice malt syrup and your milk of choice.
   Easy, quick and delicious.

5 minute cacao mousse

SERVES 4 ⊗ R + VGN + DF + GF + RSF + NF

4 small ripe avocados
4 medjool dates, pitted
55 g (2 oz/½ cup) raw cacao powder
125 ml (4 fl oz/½ cup) coconut milk
80 ml (2½ fl oz/⅓ cup) rice malt syrup
2 tablespoons melted coconut oil
1 teaspoon natural vanilla extract
1 tablespoon mesquite powder

Place all the ingredients in a food processor and blitz until smooth. Pour into four serving glasses and enjoy.

Coated in raw chocolate, these luscious coconut balls transport me to an island oasis complete with sand, palm trees, sunny skies and crystal-clear waters. Made with simple ingredients, including coconut, cashews and rice malt syrup, Coco balls are as clean as they come. Pure paradise.

Coco balls

MAKES 16 ✪ R + VGN + DF + GF + RSF

Drain the cashews and place in a food processor. Add the coconut cream, coconut oil, rice malt syrup and 135 g (4¾ oz/1½ cups) desiccated coconut. Process until the mixture is fairly smooth and sticky.

Scrape the mixture into a bowl. Add the shredded coconut and the extra 90 g (3¼ oz/1 cup) desiccated coconut and mix well.

Roll the mixture into balls and freeze for 1–2 hours, until firm.

Whisk the chocolate coating ingredients together in a small bowl.

Place a sheet of baking paper on the kitchen bench, then set a wire baking rack on top.

Coat the balls in the chocolate mixture, by dipping them in using a fork or spoon, then place on the wire rack to allow the excess chocolate to drain off. Leave for a few minutes for the chocolate to set.

Store the coco balls in an airtight container in the fridge. They will keep for up to 2 weeks.

75 g (2½ oz/½ cup) cashews, soaked for 2–3 hours
45 ml (1½ fl oz) coconut cream
45 ml (1½ fl oz) melted coconut oil
45 ml (1½ fl oz) rice malt syrup
135 g (4¾ oz/1½ cups) desiccated coconut, plus an extra 90 g (3¼ oz/1 cup)
65 g (2½ oz/1 cup) shredded coconut

Chocolate coating
250 ml (9 fl oz/1 cup) melted coconut oil
55–85 g (2–3 oz/½–¾ cup) raw cacao powder
80–125 ml (2½–4 fl oz/⅓–½ cup) maple syrup

Sesame seeds have long been prized for their nutty flavour and nourishing oil, which is used in many traditional medicines for its healing properties. Just a handful of these tiny super seeds delivers a big hit of phenolic antioxidants, minerals, vitamins and protein.

Needless to say, these deliciously chewy sesame squares are a filling, nutritious snack. They're very quick and easy to whip up, and taste heavenly with homemade chocolate drizzled on top.

Sesame squares

MAKES 8 ✪ R + VGN + DF + GF + RSF + NF

Place the sesame seeds, coconut, rice malt syrup and coconut butter in a food processor. Pulse until the mixture is well incorporated and sticks together.

Press the mixture into a tray or slab tin, measuring about 34 x 23 cm (13½ x 9 inches) and 5 cm (2 inches) deep. Freeze for 2–3 hours, or until firm enough to slice cleanly.

Combine the chocolate swirl ingredients in a bowl and whisk until well combined. Slice the sesame mixture into squares or rectangles, and use the chocolate to make decorative patterns on top.

The sesame squares will keep in an airtight container in the fridge for up to 1 week, or in an airtight container in the freezer for 6–8 weeks.

220 g (8 oz/1½ cups) sesame seeds
45 g (1½ oz/½ cup) desiccated coconut
80 ml (2½ fl oz/⅓ cup) rice malt syrup
3 tablespoons softened coconut butter

Chocolate swirl
125 ml (4 fl oz/½ cup) melted coconut oil
85 g (3 oz/¾ cup) raw cacao powder
60 ml (2 fl oz/¼ cup) maple syrup

Decadent, creamy and so exquisitely tempting, with the chocolate and raspberry pairing together so perfectly, here's a raw cheesecake that will amaze and delight.

Made with ground cashews and coconut milk, and containing no dairy, sugar or gluten, this is one of those classic dessert cakes you'll call on over and over again.

Chocolate raspberry layer cake

SERVES 10 ✪ R + VGN + DF + GF + RSF

To make the base, blend the pecans and almonds into small pieces in a food processor. Add all the other base ingredients and process until well combined and sticky.

Press the mixture into a 20 cm (8 inch) round cake tin lined with baking paper. Freeze while making the filling.

Rinse out the food processor. To make the filling, drain the cashews and place in the processor with the rice malt syrup, cacao butter, coconut milk, vanilla and salt. Blitz until the mixture is smooth and creamy.

Remove about half the filling and set aside in a bowl.

Add the cacao powder to the filling in the processor and pulse until smooth. Spread the chocolate layer over the cake base and freeze for 1–2 hours, or until firm.

Rinse out the processor again. Return the reserved filling to the processor, add the raspberries and coconut milk and pulse until smooth.

Spread the raspberry layer over the chocolate layer and freeze for at least 3–4 hours.

When you are ready to serve, remove the cake from the cake tin and invert it onto a serving plate or platter.

To make the topping, whisk the coconut oil, cacao powder and maple syrup together in a bowl.

Arrange the raspberries over the cake and pour the chocolate mixture over the middle, allowing the chocolate to spill down the side of the cake.

This cake is best enjoyed within about 30 minutes of removing from the freezer.

If making ahead, the undecorated cake will keep in an airtight container in the freezer for 4–8 weeks; top with the fresh raspberries and drizzle with the chocolate just before serving.

Base

100 g (3½ oz/1 cup) pecans
80 g (2¾ oz/½ cup) almonds
45 g (1½ oz/½ cup) desiccated coconut
25 g (1 oz/¼ cup) raw cacao powder
60 ml (2 fl oz/¼ cup) rice malt syrup
3–4 medjool dates, pitted
⅛ teaspoon Himalayan salt

Filling

375 g (13 oz/2 cups) cashews, soaked for 4 hours
125 ml (4 fl oz/½ cup) rice malt syrup
125 ml (4 fl oz/½ cup) melted cacao butter
45 ml (1½ fl oz) coconut milk
1 teaspoon vanilla powder
⅛ teaspoon Himalayan salt
55 g (2 oz/½ cup) raw cacao powder
125 g (4½ oz/1 cup) fresh raspberries
1–2 tablespoons coconut milk

Topping

250 ml (9 fl oz/1 cup) melted coconut oil
175 g (6 oz/1½ cups) raw cacao powder
170 ml (5½ fl oz/⅔ cup) maple syrup
125 g (4½ oz/1 cup) fresh raspberries

Sure to please, this layered mocha cake is a must for your next big event or special celebration. The flavours are fabulous and the texture smooth and creamy, with buckwheat groats in the vanilla layer adding the occasional crunch.

Once assembled, you can keep the cake in the freezer and simply bring it out about half an hour prior to serving.

It's bound to become a staple in your recipe collection.

Mocha celebration cake

SERVES 14 ✖ R + VGN + DF + GF + RSF

Soak the cashews for the coffee layer, vanilla crunch layer and chocolate cream for 4 hours.

To make the base, put the almonds and pecans in a food processor and blend until small pieces form. Add the remaining base ingredients and process until well blended and sticky.

Line a 24 cm (9½ inch) square cake tin, about 5 cm (2 inches) deep, with baking paper. Press the base mixture evenly into the tin and freeze while you make the filling.

Clean out the food processor. To make the coffee layer, drain the cashews and blitz in the processor with the rice malt syrup, cacao butter and coffee, adding 1–2 tablespoons water as needed to bring the mixture together.

Pour the coffee layer over the base and freeze for 1–2 hours, or until firm enough to add the next layer.

Clean out the processor again. To make the vanilla crunch layer, drain the cashews and place in the processor with the rice malt syrup, cacao butter and vanilla powder. Blend well, adding 1–2 tablespoons water as needed to bring the mixture together. Fold the buckwheat

groats through, then pour the vanilla mixture over the coffee layer. Freeze for 1–2 hours, or until firm enough to add the next layer.

Clean the processor again, in preparation for making the chocolate cream. Drain the cashews and place in the processor with the rice malt syrup and coconut cream. Blend until smooth. Add the cacao powder and pulse until well combined.

Spread the chocolate layer over the top of the cake, then freeze for at least 3–4 hours or overnight, until all the layers are set.

When ready to serve, remove the cake from the tin and place on a serving plate or platter. Decorate with the buckwheat groats and chocolate shavings. Cut into wedges to serve.

This cake is best enjoyed within about 30 minutes of removing from the freezer.

If making ahead, the undecorated cake will keep in an airtight container in the freezer for 4–8 weeks. Top with the buckwheat groats and chocolate shavings just before serving.

activated buckwheat groats, for sprinkling

40 g (1½ oz/¼ cup) shaved sugar-free dark chocolate

Coffee layer

450 g (1 lb/3 cups) cashews, soaked

125 ml (4 fl oz/½ cup) rice malt syrup

2 tablespoons melted cacao butter

125 ml (4 fl oz/½ cup) espresso coffee

Vanilla crunch layer

300 g (10½ oz/2 cups) cashews, soaked

80 ml (2½ fl oz/⅓ cup) rice malt syrup

2 tablespoons melted cacao butter

1 teaspoon vanilla powder

90 g (3¼ oz/½ cup) activated buckwheat groats

Chocolate cream

150 g (5½ oz/1 cup) cashews, soaked

60 ml (2 fl oz/¼ cup) rice malt syrup

2 tablespoons coconut cream

1 tablespoon raw cacao powder

Base

160 g (5½ oz/1 cup) almonds

100 g (3½ oz/1 cup) pecans

90 g (3¼ oz/1 cup) desiccated coconut

2 tablespoons raw cacao powder

1 teaspoon vanilla powder

⅛ teaspoon Himalayan salt

125 ml (4 fl oz/½ cup) rice malt syrup

I thought the 'salted caramel' food phase was going to come and go in a flash… but it didn't work out that way for me, thanks to this irresistible creation, which is the perfect fusion of salty and sweet. I now have a deep and fulfilling love affair with salted caramel. And after you taste this tart, I'm sure you will too.

Salty caramel tart

SERVES 8 ✕ R + VGN + DF + GF + RSF

Start by making the base. Put the cashews and macadamias in a food processor and blend until broken down into smaller pieces. Add the buckwheat groats, coconut, rice malt syrup and dates and process until the mixture sticks together.

Press the mixture evenly into a round 22 cm (8½ inch) cake tin lined with baking paper. Place in the freezer while making the caramel filling.

Clean out the food processor. Add the caramel ingredients to the processor and blend until the mixture is completely smooth.

Spread the caramel over the base and freeze while you make the chocolate drizzle.

In a bowl, combine the cacao butter, cacao powder, maple syrup and vanilla, whisking until smooth. Drizzle the chocolate over the caramel layer, then sprinkle with the salt.

Place the tart in the freezer for 3–4 hours, or until set.

Remove from the freezer about 30 minutes before serving. Cut into slices to serve.

The tart will keep in the freezer in an airtight container for 4–6 weeks.

Base
150 g (5½ oz/1 cup) cashews
155 g (5½ oz/1 cup) macadamia nuts
90 g (3¼ oz/½ cup) activated buckwheat groats
90 g (3¼ oz/1 cup) desiccated coconut
60 ml (2 fl oz/¼ cup) rice malt syrup
10 medjool dates, pitted

Caramel
225 g (8 oz/1½ cups) medjool dates, pitted
60 ml (2 fl oz/¼ cup) melted coconut oil
125 g (4½ oz/½ cup) almond butter
125 ml (4 fl oz/½ cup) rice malt syrup
1 teaspoon vanilla powder
⅛ teaspoon Himalayan salt

Chocolate drizzle
125 ml (4 fl oz/½ cup) melted cacao butter
55 g (2 oz/½ cup) raw cacao powder
80 ml (2½ fl oz/⅓ cup) maple syrup
1 teaspoon vanilla
¼ teaspoon Himalayan salt

Raw rainbow
cheesecakes *220*

×

Chocolate caramel
swirl ice cream *224*

TREAT NIGHT

Sweetness to stay at home for

Refreshingly light, these little delights are perfectly fresh and fun. You won't believe they are made using only nourishing ingredients. The fresh fruit topping looks beautiful to the eye, but also complements the creamy, slightly tangy filling perfectly. Enjoy on a special occasion or celebration — or just because.

Raw rainbow cheesecakes

MAKES 14 ✖ R + VGN + DF + GF + RSF

To make the base, place the walnuts and almonds in a food processor and blend until broken down into small pieces. Add the buckwheat groats, coconut and salt and pulse until well combined. Add the dates and rice malt syrup and process until you have a sticky mixture.

Line a 24 cm (9½ inch) square cake tin, about 5 cm (2 inches) deep, with baking paper. Press the mixture into the tin and transfer to the fridge while you make the filling.

Clean out the processor. Drain the cashews and process with the coconut oil, coconut milk and rice malt syrup. The nuts must be broken down and the filling should be smooth, so keep processing until you achieve a smooth consistency.

Fold the vanilla and lemon juice through, then pour the filling over the base. Set in the freezer for 3–4 hours.

When ready to serve, remove from the freezer and cut into pieces. Top with the mixed fruit pieces and serve.

Without the fruit topping, the cheesecakes will keep in an airtight container in the freezer for up to 4 weeks.

Base

115 g (4 oz/1 cup) walnuts

160 g (5½ oz/1 cup) almonds

90 g (3¼ oz/½ cup) activated buckwheat groats

90 g (3¼ oz/1 cup) desiccated coconut

⅛ teaspoon Himalayan salt

150 g (5½ oz/1 cup) medjool dates, pitted

125 ml (4 fl oz/½ cup) rice malt syrup

Filling

600 g (1 lb 5 oz/4 cups) cashews, soaked for at least 4 hours

250 ml (9 fl oz/1 cup) melted coconut oil

500 ml (17 fl oz/2 cups) coconut milk

375 ml (13 fl oz/1½ cups) rice malt syrup

1–2 teaspoons vanilla powder

juice of 1 lemon

Topping

½ mango, sliced

pulp of 1 passionfruit

4 strawberries, sliced

1 kiwi fruit, sliced

½ dragonfruit, sliced

2 figs, sliced

With a chocolate cream centre, sandwiched between two raw chocolate biscuits covered in a deep chocolate coating, these raw triple-chocolate biscuits are all kinds of delicious. Keep them in the freezer for when that chocolate craving strikes.

Triple-choc biscuits

MAKES 9 ✖ R + VGN + DF + GF + RSF

To make the biscuit base, put the pecans, walnuts, coconut and buckwheat groats in a food processor and blend into small pieces. Add the cacao powder and salt and pulse until well combined. Add the dates and process until combined and sticky.

Line a tin, measuring about 34 x 23 cm (13½ x 9 inches) and 5 cm (2 inches) deep, with baking paper. Press the biscuit mixture into the tin; I spread it out to about 6–7 mm (¼ inch) in height. Freeze for at least 2–3 hours.

Clean out the food processor. Add all the chocolate filling ingredients, pour in 125 ml (4½ fl oz/½ cup) water and process until smooth. (At this point I often transfer the mix to a high-speed blender and briefly blitz it for a smoother finish.) Transfer the chocolate filling mixture to a bowl and freeze for at least 2–3 hours.

Cut the chilled biscuit base into 18 rectangular biscuits. Spread the chilled chocolate filling over half

the biscuits, then sandwich the remaining biscuits on top. Leave to set in the freezer for 2–3 hours.

Whisk the chocolate coating ingredients in a bowl until well combined. You want the mixture to be thick and creamy, so if it's a bit runny at this point, place it in the fridge for 10–20 minutes to thicken.

Place a sheet of baking paper on the kitchen bench, then set a wire baking rack on top. When the chocolate coating is nice and thick, dip the chilled biscuits into the chocolate and place on the wire rack to allow the excess chocolate to drain off.

Once all the biscuits are coated, set in the freezer for 20–30 minutes.

The biscuits will keep in an airtight container in the freezer for 4–6 weeks. Remove from the freezer 10 minutes before serving.

Biscuit base

100 g (3½ oz/1 cup) pecans

115 g (4 oz/1 cup) walnuts

45 g (1½ oz/½ cup) desiccated coconut

180 g (6 oz/1 cup) activated buckwheat groats

2 tablespoons raw cacao powder

⅛ teaspoon Himalayan salt

150 g (5½ oz/1 cup) medjool dates, pitted

Chocolate filling

300 g (10½ oz/2 cups) cashews, soaked overnight

125 ml (4½ fl oz/½ cup) melted coconut oil

2 tablespoons coconut butter, softened

250 ml (9 fl oz/1 cup) rice malt syrup

25 g (1 oz/¼ cup) raw cacao powder

Chocolate coating

80 g (2¾ oz/⅔ cup) raw cacao powder

250 ml (9 fl oz/1 cup) melted coconut oil

125 ml (4½ fl oz/½ cup) maple syrup

½ teaspoon carob powder (optional)

LOVE YOURSELF
ENOUGH TO
CHOOSE HEALTHY

*No need for fancy ice cream makers or special mixers —
all you need are some basic wholefood ingredients and a
high-speed blender for this raw vegan ice cream, swirled
with creamy dreamy chocolate caramel. Apart from
soaking the cashews and dates, it is very quick to prepare,
and has a fabulous flavour and texture. Get your blender
out and give it a go. But make sure you're on your own:
it's a little too good to share!*

Chocolate caramel swirl ice cream

SERVES 8 ❁ R + VGN + DF + GF + RSF

For the chocolate ice cream, drain and rinse your cashews and set aside. Add the coconut cream and coconut oil to your blender and whiz together. Add the cashews, dates, cacao powder, vanilla and xanthan gum and blend until completely smooth. Transfer to a bowl, stir the cacao nibs and chocolate pieces through and set aside.

For the caramel ice cream, drain and rinse your cashews and set aside. Clean out your blender. Add the coconut cream and coconut oil to the blender and whiz together. Add the cashews and remaining ingredients and blend until completely smooth.

To create the swirled pattern, place about one-third of the chocolate ice cream in the bottom of an ice cream container, or a loaf (bar) tin measuring about 24 x 13 cm (9½ x 5 inches), and about 6 cm (2½ inches) deep.

Pour one-third of the caramel ice cream over the top.

Top with another one-third of the chocolate ice cream, then another one-third of the caramel. Repeat with the remaining ice cream flavours, to create the final layer.

Cover with plastic wrap and freeze for 4–5 hours or overnight, until firm.

When serving the ice cream, depending on how long it has been in the freezer, it may be a little hard to scoop. If so, place it in the fridge for about 30 minutes before serving, so it can soften.

The ice cream will keep in the freezer for up to 4 weeks.

Chocolate ice cream

300 g (10½ oz/2 cups) cashews, soaked
   overnight
375 g (13 oz/1½ cups) coconut cream
60 ml (2 fl oz/¼ cup) melted coconut oil
110 g (4 oz/¾ cup) pitted medjool dates,
   soaked for 2 hours
25 g (1 oz/¼ cup) raw cacao powder
1 teaspoon vanilla powder
¼ teaspoon xanthan gum
30 g (1 oz/¼ cup) cacao nibs
35 g (1¼ oz/¼ cup) chopped dark
   chocolate

Caramel ice cream

300 g (10½ oz/2 cups) cashews, soaked
   overnight
310 g (11 oz/1¼ cups) coconut cream
60 ml (2 fl oz/¼ cup) melted coconut oil
110 g (4 oz/¾ cup) pitted medjool dates,
   soaked for 2 hours
2 tablespoons tahini
2 tablespoons almond butter
1 tablespoon mesquite powder
1 teaspoon vanilla powder
⅛ teaspoon Himalayan salt
¼ teaspoon xanthan gum

How I love finding these stashed away in the freezer. They are the ideal treat on a hot day — in summer I have to make them on high rotation to keep the family happy. Play around with other flavour combinations by experimenting with different berries.

Creamy blueberry & lemon ice pops

MAKES 6 ✪ R + VGN + DF + GF + RSF + NF

Blueberry layer

280 g (10 oz/1 cup) coconut yoghurt, or other
   non-dairy yoghurt
1 tablespoon lemon juice
1 tablespoon rice malt syrup
75 g (2½ oz/½ cup) fresh or frozen blueberries

Lemon layer

560 g (1 lb 4 oz/2 cups) coconut yoghurt
1 tablespoon lemon juice
1 tablespoon rice malt syrup
1 teaspoon natural vanilla extract

Place the ingredients for the blueberry layer in a high-speed blender and whiz until smooth. Pour the mixture into six iceblock (popsicle/ice lolly) moulds, then freeze for 2–3 hours, until firm.

Clean out the blender, add all the lemon layer ingredients and whiz until smooth. Pour the mixture into the moulds, over the blueberry layer. Freeze for 3–4 hours, or until set.

The ice pops will keep in the freezer for 2–4 weeks.

When ready to serve, run the iceblock moulds under hot water and they will slide out easily. Enjoy immediately.

This tangy tart is one of my favourite entertaining treats. It's simple, light and incredibly refreshing. Think of summertime, long lunches and good company. Made with potassium-rich avocados and detoxifying limes, it also boasts a superior nutritional profile. Another reason to include this showstopper at your next special event.

Tangy lime tart

SERVES 8 ✪ R + VGN + DF + GF + RSF

Line a 25 cm (10 inch) round cake tin with baking paper.

Put the cashew nuts in a food processor and chop into small pieces. Add all the other crust ingredients and blend until the mixture is combined and sticky.

Press the mixture into the base of the cake tin and refrigerate while making the filling.

Clean out the food processor. Place all the filling ingredients in the processor and blend until smooth. Pour the filling over the crust and freeze overnight, or until set.

The tart will keep in an airtight container in the freezer for 4–6 weeks. Remove from the freezer 1–2 hours before serving.

Decorate with the lime slices and lime zest before cutting into wedges.

Crust
300 g (10½ oz/2 cups) cashews
90 g (3¼ oz/1 cup) desiccated coconut
75 g (2½ oz/½ cup) medjool dates, pitted
60 ml (2 fl oz/¼ cup) rice malt syrup
1 teaspoon vanilla powder
2 tablespoons lime juice
pinch of Himalayan salt

Filling
flesh from 4 large ripe avocados
125 ml (4½ fl oz/½ cup) lime juice (you'll need about 5 limes)
grated zest of 8 limes
125 ml (4½ fl oz/½ cup) rice malt syrup
1 teaspoon vanilla powder
pinch of Himalayan salt

Topping
2 limes, thinly sliced
1 tablespoon lime zest

Vegies in treats — you've gotta love that. I get a huge thrill when I create a treat from a vegetable, especially a detoxifying, antioxidant-rich vegetable with a wonderful depth of flavour. Beetroot gives such a sweet, earthy kick to this cafe-style slice.

Beetroot slice

MAKES 8 ✪ R + VGN + DF + GF + RSF

Grind the pecans and walnuts into small pieces using a food processor. You don't want the nuts to turn to a powdery meal, so keep watch and stop processing when the nuts have been chopped into small pieces.

Add the dates and rice malt syrup and process until the mixture is nice and sticky.

Squeeze the grated beetroot to drain off the excess water. The beetroot needs to be dry, otherwise your slice will be soggy.

Add the beetroot to the food processor and pulse until just combined. Add the ginger and pulse again, then add the coconut and process until all the ingredients are well combined.

Line a tray or slab tin, measuring about 34 x 23 cm (13½ x 9 inches) and 5 cm (2 inches) deep, with baking paper. Evenly press the mixture into the tray, then place in the freezer while preparing the icing.

Clean out your food processor. To make the icing, put the dates in the processor with 185 ml (6 fl oz/ ¾ cup) water and blend until smooth and paste-like. Remove from the processor and set aside.

Drain the cashews and blend in the processor with the lemon juice until creamy. Add all the other icing ingredients and blend until smooth, then add the date mixture and blend again.

Spread the icing over the chilled beetroot slice and decorate with lemon slices and cacao nibs. Cut into slices to serve.

This slice is best stored in the fridge in an airtight container and enjoyed within 3 days.

100 g (3½ oz/1 cup) pecans
115 g (4 oz/1 cup) walnuts
10 medjool dates, pitted
60 ml (2 fl oz/¼ cup) rice malt syrup
3 beetroot (beets), peeled and finely grated
1 teaspoon grated fresh ginger
180 g (6 oz/2 cups) desiccated coconut
lemon slices, to garnish
cacao nibs, to garnish

Chocolate buttercream icing
150 g (5½ oz/1 cup) medjool dates, pitted
2 tablespoons cashew nuts, soaked in water for at least 2 hours
juice of 1 lemon
25 g (1 oz/¼ cup) raw cacao powder
1 tablespoon cashew butter
2 tablespoons melted cacao butter
⅛ teaspoon Himalayan salt
½ teaspoon vanilla powder

INDEX

Published in 2017 by Murdoch Books, an imprint of Allen & Unwin

Murdoch Books Australia
83 Alexander Street,
Crows Nest NSW 2065
Phone: +61 (0)2 8425 0100
murdochbooks.com.au
info@murdochbooks.com.au

Murdoch Books UK
Ormond House,
26–27 Boswell Street,
London, WC1N 3JZ
Phone: +44 (0) 20 8785 5995
murdochbooks.co.uk
info@murdochbooks.co.uk

For Corporate Orders & Custom Publishing contact our business
development team at salesenquiries@murdochbooks.com.au

Publisher: Corinne Roberts
Editorial Manager: Jane Price
Design Manager: Vivien Valk
Designer: Madeleine Kane
Editor: Katri Hilden

Styling: David Morgan
Food assistant: Grace Campbell
Background illustrations: Bubblefish
Production Manager: Rachel Walsh

Photography © Petrina Tinslay, pages 4-5, 8-9, 10-11, 12-13, 14-15, 16-17,
18-19, 20, 22-23, 24-25, 35, 38-39, 48-49, 51, 52-53, 55, 56-57, 64-65,
66-67, 68-69, 72-73, 74-75, 77, 78-79, 85, 86-87, 89, 90-91, 97, 99, 100-01,
107, 108-09, 111, 112-13, 121, 123, 124-25, 129, 132-33, 139, 145, 146-47,
154-55, 157, 158-59, 192-93, 201, 218-19
Photography © Sneh Roy, pages 27, 28-29, 31, 33, 37, 43, 44-45, 47, 81, 83,
95, 105, 107, 127, 131, 143, 153, 161, 163, 165, 166-67, 169, 170-71, 172-3,
175, 177, 178-79, 181, 183, 185, 186-87, 189, 190-91, 202-03, 205, 206-07,
209, 211, 212-13, 215, 217, 227, 229
Photography © Omid Daghighi, front cover and page 2
Photography © Taline Gabrielian, pages 6, 60, 116, 140, 196, 222,
and back cover

Text © Taline Gabrielian 2017
Design © Murdoch Books 2017

ISBN 978 1 74336 901 2 Australia
ISBN 978 1 74336 917 3 UK
A cataloguing-in-publication entry is available from the catalogue
of the National Library of Australia at nla.gov.au
A catalogue record for this book is available from the British Library

Colour reproduction by Splitting Image Colour Studio Pty Ltd, Clayton, Victoria
Printed by C&C Offset Printing, China

MEASURES GUIDE: We have used Australian 20 ml (4 teaspoon) tablespoon
measures. If you are using a smaller European 15 ml (3 teaspoon) tablespoon,
add an extra teaspoon of the ingredient for each tablespoon specified.

DISCLAIMER: The author and publisher claim no responsibility to any person or
entity for any liability, loss, or damage caused or alleged to be caused directly
or indirectly as a result of the use, application or interpretation of the material
in this book.

Reprinted 2017 (twice)